Learning to Stay

LEARNING TO STAY

Navigating College and Persisting with Purpose

Dr. Daniel E. Haupt

Learning to Stay: Navigating College and Persisting with Purpose

Published in the United States of America
First Edition
ISBN: 979-8-9946336-1-8

Student stories are drawn from the author's doctoral research. Names and identifying details have been changed to protect privacy.

For every first-generation student who chose to stay.

And for Millicent, who taught me what persistence looks like.

CONTENTS

DEDICATION

To every first-generation college student
who has ever wondered if they truly belong—
you do.

To my family,
whose unwavering support
has made all my work possible.

And to the students
who inspire this work every day.

Acknowledgments

This book exists because of the countless first-generation college students who shared their stories, struggles, and triumphs over the years. Your courage in navigating uncharted territory inspired every page. Thank you for trusting me with your experiences.

I am deeply grateful to my family, whose partnership and support has been the foundation of everything I've accomplished. Your patience during the many late nights of writing, your thoughtful feedback on early drafts, and your unwavering belief in this project kept me going when the work felt overwhelming.

The educators, advisors, and student affairs professionals who work tirelessly to support first-generation students deserve special recognition. Your daily work brings these principles to life in ways that humble me. This book is as much yours as it is mine.

I extend my gratitude to the researchers whose work forms the scholarly foundation of this book. The citations throughout these pages represent decades of dedicated study into what helps students succeed. I stand on the shoulders of giants.

To the academic advisors, professors, and student affairs professionals who reviewed early chapters and provided invaluable feedback, your insights made this book immeasurably better. Special thanks to those who shared their own experiences as first-generation students and professionals.

Finally, to every first-generation student who reads this book: you are the reason it exists. Your success matters—not just to you and your family, but to every student who will follow in your footsteps. May these pages serve you well on your journey.

Daniel E. Haupt, PhD, EdD
Denver, Colorado
2026

INTRODUCTION

Why This Book Exists and Who It's For

"I wish someone had given me a guidebook when I started college. Not the orientation packet – but a real guide that understood what it was like to be the first in my family to do this. Something that told me it was okay to feel lost, that explained the unwritten rules everyone else seemed to know, and that reminded me I belonged here even when I doubted it."
—First-generation college student

If you're reading this book, there's a good chance you are a first-generation college student—or someone who cares deeply about helping first-generation students succeed.

Either way, welcome.

This book was written specifically for you.

Being the first in your family to attend college often means navigating unfamiliar systems without a map. You may be excited, proud, and hopeful—while also feeling uncertain, overwhelmed, or unsure whether you truly belong. Many first-generation students describe feeling like everyone else received instructions they somehow missed.

This book exists because those feelings are not personal shortcomings. They are structural realities.

College runs on hidden rules. Unspoken expectations. Assumptions about knowledge students are supposed to already have. Students who grow up around higher education often absorb these norms without realizing it. First-generation students are expected to figure them out on the fly—often while balancing financial pressure, family responsibilities, and high expectations.

The goal of this book is not to "fix" you. It's to make the system more visible.

You will not find empty motivation or unrealistic promises here. Instead, you will find research-backed strategies, honest reflection, and practical tools designed to help you stay engaged, persist through difficulty, and build a path that works for your life.

This book is also written for the people who support first-generation students—advisors, faculty, student affairs professionals, and family members who want to understand what this journey actually feels like. The more people who understand the realities first-gen students face, the stronger the support systems we can build together.

Most importantly, this book is designed to be useful.

Every chapter ends with reflection questions and action steps called **The Huddle**. These are not throwaway discussion prompts. They are intentionally designed to help you apply what you're reading to your own experience.

The goal is not simply to inform you, but to help you do something differently, something that increases your chances of not just staying enrolled but staying well.

Why Being First-Gen Is Different

Let's be clear about something important from the very start: being a first-generation college student doesn't mean you're less prepared, less capable, or less deserving of success than anyone else on campus. What it means is that you're starting from a different place than many of your peers—not a worse place, just a different one with its own unique strengths and challenges.

Students whose parents attended college often arrive with invisible advantages they may not even recognize. They've absorbed knowledge about how college works through years of dinner table conversations, campus visits during childhood, and watching their parents navigate professional careers that required higher education. They know what office hours are and that you're supposed to use them. They understand that a syllabus is both a contract and a roadmap for success. They've learned that asking for help is a sign of strategic intelligence, not weakness or failure.

> *"My roommate's parent went to the same university we were attending. They knew which professors to avoid, which dining halls had the best food, and how to navigate the financial aid office when problems came up. I didn't even know there was a financial aid office separate from admissions until my second semester when I almost lost my funding."*
>
> *—First-generation college student*

None of this means continuing-generation students have it easy—they face their own significant challenges. But it does mean that as a first-gen student, you may need to be more intentional about learning things that others picked up unconsciously over years of exposure. This book aims to make that hidden curriculum visible and accessible to you.

At the same time, being first-gen comes with real strengths that often go unrecognized. You've likely developed resilience, resourcefulness, and determination that many of your peers haven't had to cultivate. You bring perspectives and experiences that enrich classroom discussions and campus life. You understand things about hard work, sacrifice, and the real stakes of education that some students who've had easier paths may not fully grasp.

The goal isn't to become like continuing-generation students. The goal is to develop the knowledge and skills you need to succeed while maintaining the authentic identity and valuable perspective you bring to campus.

What This Book Offers

This book brings together three things that rarely appear in the same place: the voices of real first-generation students who have navigated the challenges you're facing, research-based strategies proven to help students succeed, and practical, actionable guidance you can apply immediately to your own situation.

Throughout these pages, you'll hear from students who understand your experience because they've lived it themselves. Their stories, struggles, and insights appear in their own words, offering both validation that you're not alone and wisdom from those who've been where you are. These aren't sanitized success stories that skip over the hard parts, they're honest accounts of what it really takes to persist. All identifying information has been removed to protect student privacy.

You'll also find summaries of the most relevant research on college student success—not to bore you with academic jargon, but to show you that the strategies recommended here actually work according to careful study. When I tell you that a particular approach helps students succeed, it's not just my opinion or a guess, it's backed by evidence from researchers who've dedicated their careers to understanding what makes a difference.

Most importantly, this book is designed to be genuinely useful in your daily life. Every chapter ends with reflection questions and action steps called 'The Huddle.' These aren't throwaway discussion questions—they're carefully designed to help you apply what you've read to your specific situation. The goal isn't just to inform you but to help you actually do something different, something that will increase your chances of not just surviving college but truly thriving in it.

Who Should Read This Book

This book was written primarily for first-generation college students at any stage of their journey—whether you're still in high school thinking about college, a freshman feeling overwhelmed by everything that's new, a sophomore questioning whether this is the right path, or an upperclassman preparing for what comes after graduation. The principles in these pages apply across your entire college experience and beyond.

> *"I found a book similar to this during my junior year and wished desperately that I'd had it as a freshman. But honestly, a lot of it was still incredibly helpful even that late in my college career. Some things you're just not ready to hear or apply until you've lived through certain experiences first."*
>
> *—First-generation college student*

This book is also valuable for anyone who supports first-gen students: academic advisors looking for resources to share with their advisees, faculty members wanting to understand the first-gen experience better so they can be more effective teachers and mentors, student affairs professionals designing programs and services, and family members who want to understand what their student is going through even if they can't fully relate from personal experience.

The more people who understand what first-generation students face, the better the support systems we can build together. If you're reading this as someone who supports first-gen students rather than as a first-gen student yourself, I hope these pages give you insight, empathy, and practical ideas you can use in your important work.

How to Use This Book

You can read this book straight through from beginning to end, following the natural progression from understanding your identity to building your foundation to navigating your path to completing your journey. Or you can jump directly to the chapters most relevant to your current situation and pressing needs. Each chapter is designed to stand on its own while also building on themes and concepts from earlier sections.

However you choose to read it, I encourage you to engage actively rather than passively. Keep a pen handy or use the notes app on your phone. When something resonates with you, mark it so you can return to it later. When you disagree with something, note that too—your disagreement might reveal something important about your own situation and perspective.

The reflection questions at the end of each chapter—called 'The Huddle'—are designed for both individual reflection and group conversation with others. Consider working through them with a friend, a study group, an advisor, or a mentor. There's something powerful about processing these ideas in community with others who are navigating similar challenges or who want to support you on your journey.

Most importantly, act on what you learn. Knowledge without application is just entertainment. It might be interesting or even inspiring, but it doesn't change your life. The students who benefit most from books like this are the ones who actually try the strategies, reflect honestly on what works for them, and keep iterating until they find their own personalized path to success.

What's Ahead

In the chapters that follow, we'll explore the essential elements of college success for first-generation students. The book is organized into four parts that mirror the journey you're taking.

Part One, 'Understanding Your Journey,' examines identity and purpose in Chapter 1, understanding how college transforms you and why having a clear sense of why you're here matters for persistence. Chapter 2 dives into learning strategies that actually work according to cognitive science research, helping you study smarter rather than just harder.

Part Two, 'Building Your Foundation,' explores the habits, relationships, and resilience that sustain you over the long haul. Chapter 3 focuses on building habits and systems that keep you on track when motivation inevitably fades. Chapter 4 addresses the relationships and connections that will support you through challenges and setbacks. Chapter 5 examines resilience—how to persist through the difficult times that every college student faces.

Part Three, 'Navigating Your Path,' covers the practical aspects of your journey. Chapter 6 helps you clarify your direction and make decisions about your academic and professional path. Chapter 7 explores the legacy you're creating as a first-gen student and your broader impact on those who follow. Chapter 8 covers practical navigation skills for managing money, health, and campus bureaucracy. Chapter 9 maps the distinct challenges and opportunities of each year from freshman through senior year.

Part Four, 'Completing Your Journey,' prepares you for success both now and after graduation. Chapter 10 introduces artificial intelligence as a powerful learning tool available to you around the clock. Chapter 11 focuses on career preparation, graduate school decisions, and life after college. And Chapter 12 brings everything together into your personalized action plan for success.

The book concludes with a final message about taking everything you've learned into the rest of your life, followed by references for those who want to explore the research further.

A Personal Word

I wrote this book because I believe deeply in your capacity to succeed—to grow, to contribute, to overcome obstacles, and to become whoever you want to become. College is genuinely hard for everyone, and it presents particular challenges for first-generation students that others may not see or understand. But those challenges are not insurmountable. With the right strategies, the right support, and the right mindset, you can absolutely thrive.

The title of this book—'Learning to Stay'—captures something essential about the first-generation college experience. Staying in college when you could leave, when others have left, when everything feels overwhelming and quitting seems like the sensible option—that's a skill that can be learned. It requires developing certain habits, building certain relationships, and cultivating certain ways of thinking about yourself and your journey.

Research consistently shows that one of the biggest differences between students who graduate and students who don't, is not intelligence or preparation, it is persistence through difficulty. It's the ability to encounter setbacks and keep going anyway. It's learning to stay when leaving would be easier.

That's what this book is ultimately about. Not just surviving college, but developing the knowledge, skills, relationships, and mindset that allow you to thrive—to get everything you came for and more. To become not just a college graduate but a person who has grown through the experience in ways that will serve you for the rest of your life.

You belong here. You have what it takes. Let's learn how to stay —and how to flourish while you do.

...

Your journey is unique, but you don't have to walk it alone. Let's begin.

A Personal Word from the Author

This book is meant to be read slowly, reflectively, and conversationally. It is not a checklist to complete, but a guide to engage with. The college journey is deeply personal, and the purpose of this book is to serve as a research-informed, compassionate companion along the way.

Throughout these pages, we explore the hidden curriculum of higher education, the internal landscapes of identity and purpose, and the practical strategies that help students not just survive college but truly thrive. While the principles in this book are grounded in decades of research on student success, they are written for the student who is living that research every day.

Many of the student stories shared here come from my own doctoral research on the persistence of first-generation college students. Others reflect years of listening to students describe what it feels like to navigate systems that were not built with them in mind.

My perspective in this book comes from both research and practice. I have served as a retention specialist and academic advisor supporting CIS and Business Intelligence majors, and my doctoral research examined the persistence of first-generation college students. I hold a Doctor of Education in Organizational Leadership and have spent much of my career working with students navigating college as the first in their families to do so.

My connection to this work is also personal. I was a first-generation college student who left college during my third year after accepting what I believed was my dream job. At the time, it felt like success. But twelve years later, I returned and finished what I had started. By the time I came back, persistence had matured in me. I understood staying differently.

During that same season, something remarkable happened. Three of my young adult children and I were first-generation college students together, learning the hidden rules of higher education at the same time. In our family, persistence became something we practiced together. We were learning how to stay.

Over time I came to understand something that research later confirmed: staying is not passive. Staying is courage. Staying is strategy. And for many first-generation students, staying becomes legacy in motion.

My hope is that you will recognize parts of your own story in these pages. And in doing so, you will discover new ways to learn, to persist, and ultimately to stay.

— Dr. Daniel E. Haupt
Denver, Colorado

Figure 1

The Learning to Stay Roadmap for First-Generation College Success

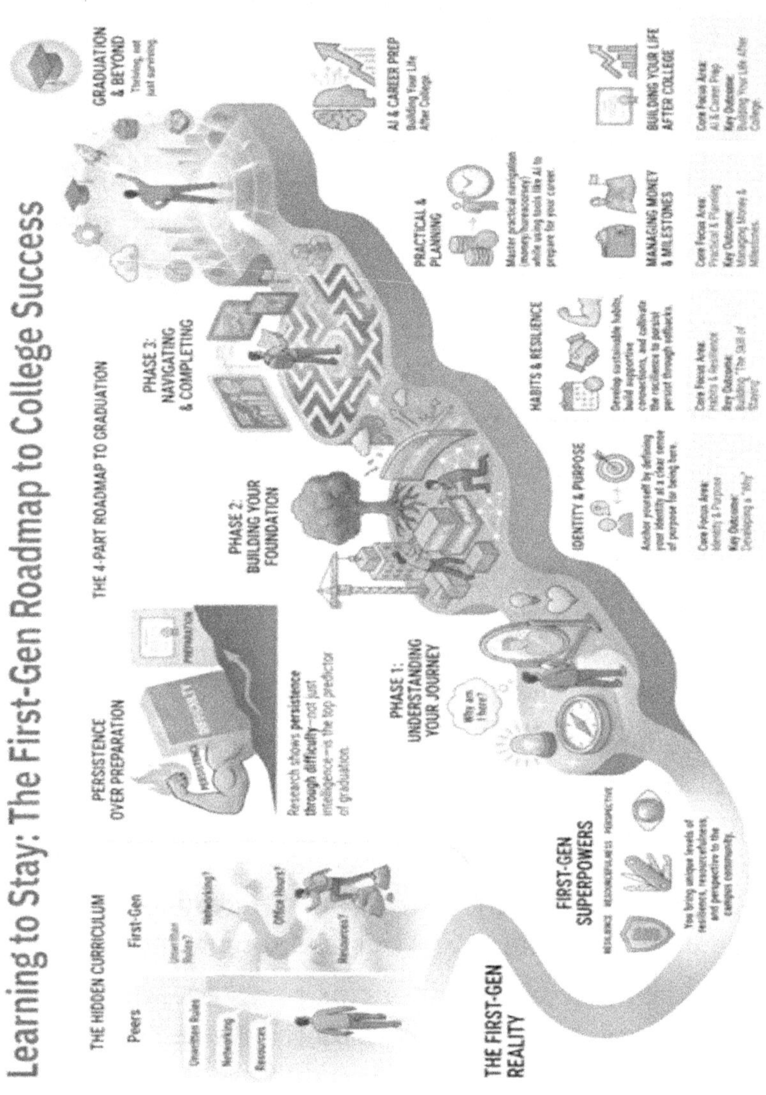

A visual overview of the Learning to Stay framework. The model illustrates the journey first-generation students navigate from encountering the hidden curriculum of college through identity development, resilience, practical navigation, and career preparation.

CHAPTER 1

Identity, Purpose, and the College Journey

> *"Sometimes I felt caught between two worlds—my family's expectations and my new life as a college student. I wasn't sure which version of myself was the real one, or if I had to choose between them."*
>
> *—First-generation college student*

Here's something no one tells you when you start college: it's not just about getting a degree. It's about becoming a new person. Not better or worse—just different. Changed in ways you can't predict when you first walk onto campus or sit down in your first class.

The student who opens this chapter may feel caught between two worlds. That feeling is real. I've heard it from hundreds of students over the years. And it's not a sign that something is wrong with you. It means college is doing what it's supposed to do. It's stretching you. It's pushing you to grow in ways that feel uncomfortable at first but lead somewhere important.

But no one prepared you for this part. Orientation showed you where to eat and how to sign up for classes. It covered the basics of getting settled. What it didn't cover was the deeper stuff. It didn't warn you about the identity questions that hit in your second year. It didn't explain the guilt you might feel when your family doesn't understand your new life.

That's what this chapter is about. I want to give you a map for the inner journey of college—the one that happens alongside classes and exams and group projects. When you understand what's really happening inside you, the confusion makes more sense. The struggles feel less scary. And you realize you're not the only one going through this. You're not even close to being alone.

I've worked with students for over forty years. I've watched them arrive uncertain and leave transformed. I've done research on what helps them succeed and what trips them up. And here's what I know for sure: the degree matters, but so does the person holding it. College changes who you are. That's actually the whole point of being here.

Let me say that again because it's important: becoming a different person is not a side effect of college. It's the main event. The classes teach you content. But the whole experience—the people you meet, the challenges you face, the questions you wrestle with—shapes who you become. That's the real education.

College Changes You—And That's the Point

For years, researchers have studied how people change during college. What they found is pretty amazing. College doesn't just make you smarter. It changes how you think, how you connect with people, how you see yourself, and what you believe matters in life. It shapes you as a whole person, not just your brain.

Think about it for a moment. You show up at eighteen or twenty-two or thirty-five. You're one person, shaped by your family, your neighborhood, and your experiences up to that point. A few years later, you're different. Still you at the core—but you've grown in ways that go far beyond passing tests and writing papers.

Two researchers, Arthur Chickering and Linda Reisser, spent years figuring out exactly how students change. They found seven main areas of growth. I'm going to walk you through all seven because I think they'll help you make sense of what you're going through right now.

These aren't stages you complete in order, like levels in a

video game where you beat one and move to the next. They're more like different directions you're growing all at once. You might do great in one area while struggling in another. That's normal. That's actually how growth works for everyone.

As you read through these seven areas, notice which ones feel true for you right now. Which ones describe exactly where you are in this moment? That recognition is valuable. It means you're starting to understand your own journey. And understanding is the first step toward taking charge of where you go next.

The conceptual structure of Chickering and Reisser's framework is illustrated in Figure 2, which presents the developmental vectors that collectively shape student identity formation and influence persistence in higher education environments.

Chickering's Seven Vectors of Development

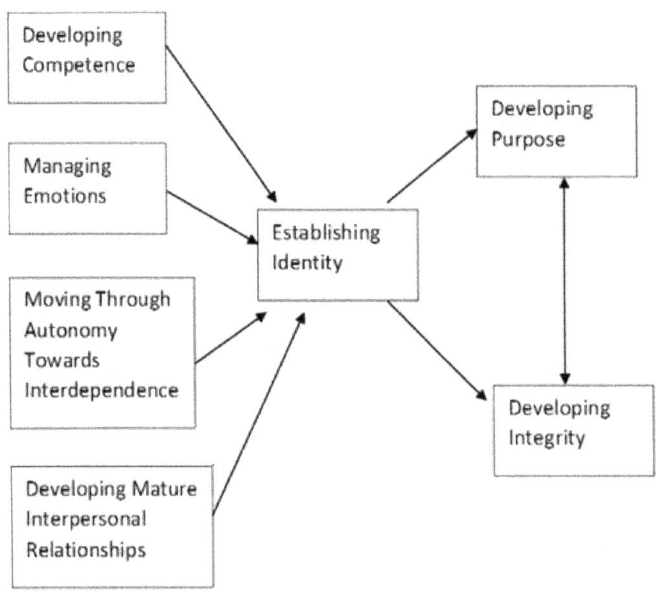

Figure 2. Chickering's Seven Vectors of Student Development

Adapted from Chickering and Reisser (1993). The seven vectors represent key developmental processes through which college students build competence, identity, purpose, and integrity.

Getting Good at This

The first area is about building skills—getting good at the things college asks you to do. This means writing papers that make sense. Thinking through problems step by step. Understanding ideas that seem hard at first. Managing your time so you're not always running behind. Working with others even when it's frustrating. Speaking up in class when you have something important to say.

But competence is more than just a list of skills you can check off. It's about building confidence—that deep feeling that you can handle what comes at you. When you push through something hard and make it to the other side, when you fail and find the strength to get back up, when you figure out something that seemed impossible at first—that builds something in you that no one can ever take away.

Here's the thing nobody warns you about: what worked in high school might not work in college. They're different games with different rules. Many students who were stars in high school hit college and find that their old ways don't work anymore. The strategies that got them straight A's suddenly fall flat. This can feel like a personal failure, but it's not.

> *"I didn't know how to study right until my second year. Before that, I felt behind everyone else. In high school, I could skim the chapter the night before and ace the test. That strategy crashed and burned in college."*
>
> *—First-generation college student*

Sound familiar? If you've had that experience, you're in good company. The good news from that student's story is that she figured it out. It took until second year, which felt like forever at the time. But eventually the skills clicked into place. I saw this pattern over and over in my research. Students struggle at first. They feel lost.

If you're in the hard part right now, I want you to hear this clearly: your struggles don't mean you don't belong here. They might just mean you're still building skills that some of your classmates got a head start on. The gap is real, but it can be closed. It's not permanent. It's not a reflection of your worth or your potential.

A 2021 study by Alzen and colleagues found that students who got academic coaching did better in their classes and were more likely to come back the next year. What does this mean? It means these skills can be learned. You're not stuck with whatever approach you brought from high school. With the right help and the right strategies, you can build what you need.

There's another kind of skill that matters just as much: knowing how college actually works. Things like knowing that professors want you to visit their office hours—you're not bothering them by showing up. Or figuring out what 'recommended reading' really means. Or learning how to email a professor without sounding weird. Or knowing where to find help when you need it and how to ask for it without feeling embarrassed.

> *"My first semester, I didn't know professors had office hours. I thought they were too busy and too important for students like me. When I finally worked up the nerve to go, I found out they actually wanted to help."*
>
> *—First-generation college student*

If your parents went to college, they probably taught you these hidden rules without anyone realizing it. It came up naturally in family talks over many years. But if you're first-gen? You're figuring it out as you go, often by making mistakes that feel embarrassing at the time but teach you something valuable.

Research by Toutkoushian and colleagues in 2021 showed that first-gen students navigate college differently. Not because they're less smart—that's definitely not it. It's because they're learning two things at once: the course material that everyone has to learn and the hidden rules of college life that some students absorbed at home over many years. That's harder.

Riding the Emotional Waves

College is an emotional ride. Stress. Excitement. Loneliness. Pride. Fear. Joy. Homesickness. Doubt. Sometimes all of these show up in the same week, or even the same day. Learning to handle all these feelings is a huge part of growing during these years.

Let me be clear about what managing emotions does not mean. It doesn't mean stuffing them down or pretending you're fine when you're falling apart inside. That strategy doesn't work anyway—the feelings just leak out somewhere else, often in ways that make things worse. Emotions aren't enemies to defeat. They're information. They tell you what's going on inside you.

Managing emotions means three things. First, noticing what you actually feel instead of pushing it away or pretending it's not there. Second, understanding why you feel that way—what triggered it. Third, finding healthy ways to deal with it instead of being controlled by it or acting it out in ways you regret later.

For first-gen students, the emotional load is often heavier than what other students carry. You might feel the weight of your family's hopes on your shoulders. Everything they sacrificed, all their dreams for your future—it's riding on you. When you struggle, you're not just letting yourself down. You might feel guilty, like you're failing everyone who believed in you and worked hard to get you here.

> *"I always worried about failing because my family expected me to make it. That pressure sat in the back of my mind all the time. Every test felt like life or death."*
>
> *—First-generation college student*
>
> *"Being the first in my family to go to college carries a lot of weight. I felt like everyone's dreams were sitting right on my shoulders. When I struggled, it wasn't just about me."*
>
> *—First-generation college student*

That pressure is real. Don't let anyone tell you to just get over it or that you're being dramatic. But I also want you to know this: those feelings are normal. You're not weak for having them. You're not broken. You're dealing with something genuinely hard that a lot of your classmates don't have to face.

You might also feel isolated because the people who love you most can't really understand what you're going through day to day. They haven't experienced college themselves. They want to help, but they don't know how. That disconnect can feel lonely even when you're surrounded by people who care about you deeply.

Almost two-thirds of the students I talked to in my research said counseling services helped them a lot. Not because they were broken or had something wrong with them—but because having someone to talk to, someone outside the situation who could offer a fresh view, made everything easier to handle. These were regular students dealing with regular stress who found that professional support made a real difference in their lives.

> *"Counseling helped me see that my feelings were normal. I wasn't weak—I was just dealing with a lot and needed some support. Learning to talk*

> *about what was going on inside me made everything more manageable."*
>
> *—First-generation college student*

Research by McNaughton-Cassill and colleagues in 2021 showed that stress directly affects your grades. This isn't just in your head—it shows up in real results. Managing your emotional life isn't separate from your schoolwork—it's deeply connected to it. Taking care of your mental health is taking care of your academic success. They go together.

Standing on Your Own—While Leaning on Others

This area is about learning to stand on your own feet while also knowing when to ask for help. Here's the key insight: the goal isn't total independence where you never need anyone for anything. That sounds strong, but it's actually a trap. The real goal is balance—being able to take care of yourself and knowing when to lean on others.

Many first-gen students show up at college already pretty independent. You've handled things on your own for years. You've figured out problems that other kids just handed to their parents without thinking twice. You've navigated systems without much guidance. In some ways, you might be more self-reliant than your classmates from day one.

But college throws new challenges at you. The systems are unfamiliar. The rules are different from anything you've dealt with before. The stakes feel higher. You can't always figure it out just by being smart and working hard the way you did before.

> *"At first, I called my mom for everything. Then I realized she couldn't help me—she didn't know how college worked. She wanted to help so badly, but she just didn't have the information. I had to figure it out myself. It was scary but also kind of empowering."*

—First-generation college student

That moment—when you realize your parents can't guide you through this particular maze—is a turning point many first-gen students face. It can feel lonely and scary. But here's what I want you to understand: you don't have to do this completely alone. The goal is building new support networks at college while staying connected to your family back home.

Research by Roksa and Kinsley in 2019 found something really important: what matters most from your family isn't whether they can help with homework or explain how to pick classes. It's whether they believe in you. That emotional support —knowing your people are in your corner even when they can't help with the details—actually predicts whether students make it through to graduation.

> *"My parents don't understand what I'm studying. They can't help me with my papers or explain my assignments. But they believe in me completely. That belief keeps me going when things get hard. I call them for encouragement, not for advice."*
>
> *—First-generation college student*

So stay connected to your family even when they can't help with the specifics of college life. Their belief in you matters more than whether they understand your major. And at the same time, build new connections at school—mentors who've been where you are, friends going through the same struggles, professors who care about your success. You need both worlds working together.

Learning when to handle things yourself and when to ask for help is a skill that takes time to develop. A lot of first-gen students default to doing everything alone because that's what they've always done. But in college, asking for help isn't weakness. It's actually smart strategy. The most successful students aren't the ones who figure out everything solo. They're the ones who know how to use the resources around them.

Building Real Connections

College puts you together with people from all kinds of backgrounds. Different races. Different religions. Different views on life. Different ways of seeing the world. Learning to build real connections across these differences is a huge part of what you're developing during these years.

But this area isn't just about meeting people who are different from you. It's about depth. Can you be real with people instead of hiding behind a mask? Can you let them see the true you, including the messy parts? Can you work through conflict instead of just walking away when things get hard? Can you stick with a relationship when it gets complicated?

In my research, relationships came up again and again as one of the biggest factors in whether students made it through to graduation. Students who built real connections—with mentors, friends, and teachers—showed way more strength when things got tough. Those relationships gave them emotional support when they were struggling. They gave practical help for navigating problems. They gave accountability to keep going. They gave a reason to stay.

> *"Having a mentor who believed in me made a huge difference. She saw things in me that I couldn't see in myself. When I wanted to quit—and there were definitely times I wanted to quit—she reminded me why I started."*
>
> *—First-generation college student*

> *"I used to feel completely alone in my classes until I finally worked up the courage to form a study group. Now I have people to lean on academically and personally. We push each other to do well."*

—First-generation college student

These relationships didn't happen by accident or overnight. Many students told me they spent their first semester—or even their whole first year—feeling like outsiders. They kept to themselves. They didn't go to events. They felt like everyone else knew each other and they didn't belong.

The turning point came when they took a risk. They joined a group even though it felt awkward. They reached out to someone they didn't know. They said yes to an invitation they wanted to turn down. Those small moments of courage led to the connections that would end up sustaining them through college.

Research by Smith and Tinto in 2022 put it this way: success in college is fundamentally about relationships. It's not just about showing up to class or turning in your work on time. It's about connecting with people who are on the same journey you're on. Those connections give you both the push to keep going and the support to get through the hard times.

One more thing about relationships: as you grow and change during college, your relationships back home might feel different. Old friendships might not fit the way they used to. Family dynamics might shift. That's normal, but it can hurt. Students who handle this well don't pick one world over the other. They find ways to build bridges between both worlds instead of walls.

Figuring Out Who You Are

This is the big one—figuring out who you really are at the core. Your values. Your beliefs. What you stand for and what you won't stand for. It sounds like a simple question, but it goes deep once you start actually thinking about it.

College is like boot camp for building your identity. You run into new ideas that shake up what you always thought was true. You meet people who live completely different lives and seem perfectly happy about it. You're asked to think for yourself in ways that might feel uncomfortable at first. You encounter beliefs that challenge things your family taught you.

For first-gen students, identity work can get extra tricky. You might feel caught between who you were at home and who you're becoming at school. You might wonder if getting educated means leaving your roots behind. You might catch yourself talking differently or thinking differently and feel strange about it. You might not recognize yourself sometimes.

> *"College changed how I think about so many things—religion, politics, social issues, my whole future. It made me question beliefs I'd held my whole life without ever really examining them. I wasn't sure if I was growing or losing myself."*
>
> *—First-generation college student*

Here's what I want you to know: questioning what you believe isn't betrayal. It's actually growth. You're not leaving your family behind by learning to think for yourself. You're doing what adults do—looking at the ideas you were handed, testing them against new information, and deciding which ones you want to keep. That's how you build an identity that's truly yours.

This process can feel unsettling for a while. You might go through a period where you're not sure what you believe about anything. That in-between space is uncomfortable but also normal. Identity building involves some taking apart before you can put together something new and solid.

Research by Museus and Chang in 2021 found that students who develop a clear sense of who they are show more resilience when facing challenges. Your identity becomes an anchor. When everything else feels chaotic—when you're stressed, confused, and overwhelmed—you can come back to who you are and what you stand for. That stability helps you weather the storms.

Something powerful happens when you stop seeing your first-gen background as a problem to overcome and start seeing it as part of who you are. The challenges you've faced have built things in you—grit, street smarts, resourcefulness, a perspective that people with easier paths simply don't have. That's not a weakness to hide. That's a strength to build on.

> *"I used to feel embarrassed that my parents didn't go to college. I thought it meant something was wrong with my family. Now I'm proud of how far I've come and what I've learned through the struggle. Being first-gen is part of who I am."*
>
> *—First-generation college student*

Finding Your Why

Purpose is about the big question: why? Why are you doing this? Why are you putting yourself through all the stress and hard work of college? What keeps you going when you're tired and overwhelmed and wondering if any of it is worth the effort?

This was one of the clearest patterns I found in my research: students with a strong sense of purpose were way more likely to finish. When they knew why they were there—not just 'to get a degree' but something deeper and more personal—they could push through the hard times. Purpose was like fuel that kept them moving when everything else felt impossible.

> *"Once I knew what I wanted to do with my life, it got so much easier to stay motivated. Having a clear career goal made school feel meaningful. I could see how my classes connected to my future instead of feeling like a bunch of random hoops to jump through."*
>
> *—First-generation college student*

> *"When I saw how education connected to my future—not just getting a degree but building the actual life I wanted—my commitment to college*

got so much stronger."

—First-generation college student

Purpose is different from goals, though people often mix them up. A goal is specific: get a 3.5 GPA, graduate in four years, land a good job. Purpose is the deeper meaning underneath those goals—why they matter to you, what they connect to, what kind of life and contribution you're trying to build.

Research by Klussman and colleagues in 2021 found that purpose works best when it feels genuinely yours. Not your parents' dream for you. Not what society says you should want. Not what looks impressive on paper. Your own real sense of what matters and why you're doing this. When your goals feel authentic, they power you forward in a deeper, more lasting way.

For first-gen students, purpose often has two layers that work together. There's what you want for yourself—your own dreams and hopes for your future. And there's what you want to do for your family—to honor their sacrifices, to make their hard work mean something, to open doors for brothers, sisters, cousins, and kids who come after you. Both of these can fuel you, and they don't have to compete.

"My parents never got the chance to go to college. They worked jobs they didn't love their whole lives so I could be here. I'm doing this for them and for me. Both reasons matter."

—First-generation college student

What if you don't know your purpose yet? That's actually okay. Most people don't have it all figured out early on. Purpose usually develops over time through trying things, talking to people, and paying attention to what draws you in. What problems make you want to do something? What topics can you talk about for hours? What kind of work makes time disappear? Those reactions are clues pointing you somewhere important.

Purpose Becomes Professional Direction

Up to this point, we've talked about purpose as fuel. It's the deeper reason you're here — the "why" that keeps you going when the work feels heavy. But at some point, purpose has to move beyond inspiration. It has to shape your decisions.

Purpose cannot stay internal. It must begin to influence what you study, how you spend your time, the relationships you build, and the opportunities you pursue. Otherwise, it remains meaningful but not practical.

This is where many students get stuck. They feel a strong sense of motivation. They want to make their families proud. They want stability, impact, or opportunity. But they haven't yet translated that purpose into direction. That translation matters.

Purpose answers the question, Why am I doing this? Professional direction begins to answer, What am I building? You can have purpose without clarity, and you can chase a career without meaning. What sustains students over time is alignment between the two.

For example, a student who cares deeply about fairness may find direction in law, policy, or social work. A student who loves solving complex problems may gravitate toward engineering or research. Someone motivated by service may pursue healthcare or education. Another student may prioritize financial stability and choose a field with strong mobility and security. In each case, the profession becomes the vehicle, and purpose remains the engine. Both are necessary.

Professional direction does not require having your entire life mapped out. It simply requires a clear enough next step. Many first-generation students feel pressure to choose perfectly, especially when family sacrifice feels connected to every decision. That pressure can create paralysis. But clarity rarely appears before action. It grows through movement — through trying classes, talking with professors, testing internships, and noticing what energizes you versus what drains you.

One student once told me, “I kept waiting to feel 100 percent sure. I realized clarity came after I tried things, not before.” That realization marked a turning point. Direction developed not through certainty, but through engagement.

When your studies connect to something larger, everyday decisions become easier. Office hours feel purposeful rather than optional. An intimidating internship becomes a strategic step rather than a risk. Protecting study time becomes an investment rather than a sacrifice. Students who develop direction tend to choose electives intentionally, seek mentors aligned with their goals, and persist longer in difficult courses — not because they are more disciplined, but because they can see where they are headed.

For many first-generation students, professional direction also carries an added layer of meaning. It may include breaking cycles of instability, serving communities like the one you grew up in, or creating access for those who follow. That sense of responsibility can be powerful. But direction cannot be sustained by obligation alone. It must also include alignment and personal fulfillment. Work built only on sacrifice eventually leads to burnout. Work rooted in both impact and personal fit creates longevity.

You are not simply choosing a career. You are building a life. And once you begin to clarify that direction, your daily actions take on new meaning. If you want to become a nurse, integrity in your science courses matters now. If you want to be an engineer, your approach to problem-solving matters now. If you want to teach, the way you treat people matters now. Professional identity begins long before graduation. You are not only preparing for a role — you are practicing it.

Knowing your purpose is powerful. Clarifying your direction makes it concrete. Living in alignment with both is where real transformation happens. That alignment is what we turn to next.

Purpose in Motion: Turning Growth into Professional Capital

College is not only shaping who you are internally. It is also shaping how others will experience you professionally. Every decision you make this semester carries a dual effect. It forms your identity, and at the same time it sends signals about who you are becoming.

Most students do not realize this. They assume professional development begins after graduation, once they step into a full-time role. In reality, that process is already underway. Persistence, then, is not just about staying enrolled long enough to earn a degree. It is about building professional capital. Professional capital is the accumulation of habits, behaviors, competencies, and character traits that increase your effectiveness and credibility over time. It is what makes others trust you with responsibility. It is what allows opportunities to expand rather than contract. While a diploma signals completion, professional capital signals readiness. Your college experience is unfolding along two tracks simultaneously. On one track, you are progressing academically — completing courses, passing exams, earning credits, and moving toward graduation. On the other track, you are undergoing professional formation. You are learning to manage your time. You are strengthening communication skills. You are practicing collaboration in group projects. You are navigating disagreement. You are responding to feedback. You are developing emotional regulation and resilience under pressure.

The first track earns you a credential. The second builds credibility. Many students focus only on grades because grades are visible and measurable. But credibility forms more quietly. It develops through repeated behaviors that seem ordinary in the moment yet accumulate power over time. When you attend office hours, you are not simply clarifying an assignment. You are practicing professional communication. You are learning how to initiate contact, ask thoughtful questions, and advocate for yourself respectfully.

When you revise a paper after receiving feedback, you are doing more than improving a grade. You are developing coachability — the capacity to receive critique without defensiveness and use it to improve. In nearly every profession, that quality distinguishes those who grow from those who stagnate.

When you push through a difficult semester, you are not merely surviving. You are strengthening adaptive capacity — the ability to function under stress, adjust to changing demands, and continue moving forward despite discomfort. These moments may feel small, but they are formative. Over time, your habits become patterns. Your patterns shape how others experience you. And how others experience you becomes your professional reputation.

Employers rarely fixate on a single exam score. They pay attention to whether you can think clearly, communicate effectively, collaborate, manage feedback, and persist when situations grow complex. Those capacities are not developed in a single class. They are formed gradually through the very challenges you are navigating now.

This is how persistence becomes employability. Every class you complete moves you closer to a degree. Every disciplined choice you make builds professional capital. The question is not only whether you will graduate. It is also who you will be when you do.

Using AI to Name What You're Building

One of the challenges many students face is recognizing the professional strengths they are already developing. You may be building valuable skills without having language for them. That can make interviews feel intimidating and résumés feel thin, even when you've grown significantly.

AI can help you articulate the professional signals embedded in your academic behaviors.

The goal is not to exaggerate your experience. It is to translate it. The discipline required to complete a demanding semester, the initiative shown by visiting office hours, the resilience required to recover from a disappointing grade — all of these are professional strengths. Sometimes you simply need help naming them clearly.

You can use AI as a reflection partner. After listing your academic habits or recent behaviors, ask it to help you identify the underlying professional capacities you are developing.

For example:

Prompt:

"Help me identify the professional strengths I am building through these academic habits: [list habits]."

You might list things such as:

- Attending weekly office hours
- Revising assignments after feedback
- Managing a part-time job while taking 15 credits
- Leading a study group
- Meeting deadlines consistently
- Recovering from a low exam grade and adjusting study strategies

AI can then help you see patterns you may overlook communication skills, coachability, time management, adaptability, leadership, or follow-through. Used this way, AI becomes a tool for reflection and articulation. It helps you recognize that your growth in college is not invisible. It is measurable, transferable, and professionally meaningful.

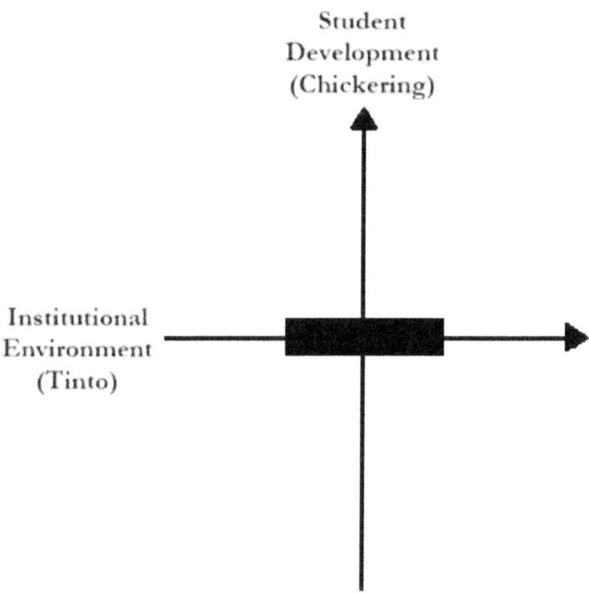

Figure 3. A conceptual model integrating Vincent Tinto's theory of institutional integration with Chickering and Reisser's student development framework. Persistence emerges through the interaction between institutional environments and the internal development of student identity.

Walking Your Talk

The last area of growth is about integrity—getting clear on your values and then actually living by them when it matters. It's about shrinking the gap between what you say you believe and what you actually do when no one is watching or when doing the right thing is hard.

College will test your integrity in big ways and small ways. You'll be tempted to cut corners—to cheat on that exam, to copy that paper, to take the easy path when no one would know. You'll face situations where doing the right thing is hard and doing the wrong thing would be so easy.

> *"College showed me so many different viewpoints —people from different religions, different politics, different backgrounds with different values. At first it completely overwhelmed me and I didn't know what to think. Over time I learned to really listen, think it through carefully, and form my own conclusions."*
>
> *—First-generation college student*

Building integrity isn't about becoming judgmental or rigid or thinking you have all the answers. It's about doing the hard work of deciding what you truly believe—and then having the courage to act on it even when it costs you something. It means becoming someone whose words and actions actually match up.

For first-gen students, integrity can get complicated. The values you learned at home might not always match what you hear at school. The way your family does things might be different from what college culture expects. Building integrity doesn't mean picking one world and rejecting the other. It means thoughtfully building your own sense of right and wrong, drawing wisdom from everything you've learned and everyone who's taught you something valuable.

Integrity also means owning your mistakes. When you mess up—and you will because you're human—it means admitting it honestly instead of making excuses or blaming someone else. That kind of honesty is hard in the moment, but it's how you build trust with others and respect for yourself over time.

Your Journey From Here

So there they are—seven areas where college is changing you right now, whether you realize it or not. Building skills. Handling emotions. Finding balance between standing alone and leaning on others. Making real connections. Figuring out who you are. Finding your purpose. Living with integrity.

You won't grow perfectly in all seven areas at once. Nobody does. You might surge ahead in one area while getting stuck in another. You might make progress and then slide backward for a while. That's normal. Growth is messy and rarely follows a straight line. Some weeks you'll feel like you're flying. Other weeks you'll wonder if you're making any progress at all. Both of those are part of the journey.

But here's what I want you to take away from this chapter: the struggles you face aren't random bad luck. They're not signs that you don't belong here or that you made a mistake coming to college. They are your education.

Research by Palmer and Maramba in 2021 shows that colleges need to do better at supporting first-gen students through this journey. The systems don't always work the way they should. But even when your school falls short, you can take ownership of your own growth. Seek out experiences that challenge you. Build relationships that support you. Pay attention to what's happening inside you, not just what shows up on your transcript.

Be patient with yourself. This transformation doesn't happen in a semester or even in a year. It takes time. Trust the process even when it feels uncertain. Give yourself permission to struggle and grow at your own pace. You're becoming someone —and that someone is going to be pretty amazing.

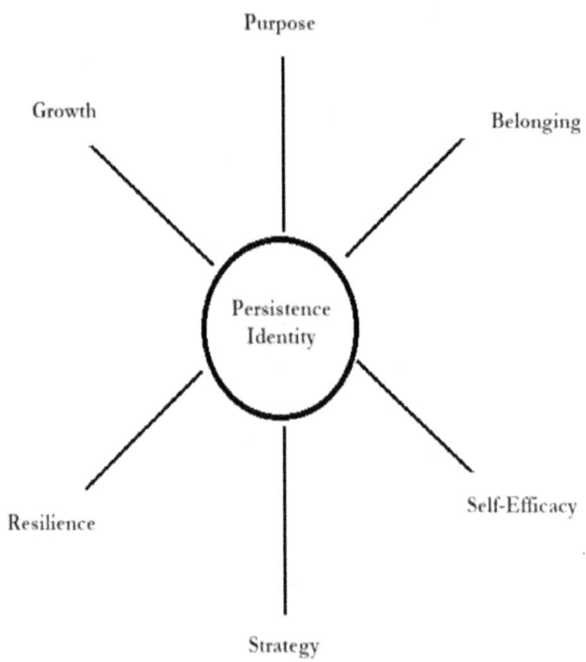

Figure 4. The Learning to Stay Persistence Model

The Learning to Stay model conceptualizes persistence as a developing identity shaped by purpose, belonging, self-efficacy, resilience, strategic action, and growth. These dimensions interact to form a persistence identity that sustains students through the college journey.

What Research Helps Us Understand

Decades of research show that college changes people in ways that go far beyond academics. The seven areas of growth —building skills, handling emotions, finding balance, making connections, establishing identity, finding purpose, and developing integrity—capture the heart of this transformation. Students who actively engage with these challenges do better in school and in life after graduation. First-gen students face extra hurdles because they're learning the hidden rules of college while also learning the content.

The Huddle

Take time to reflect on these questions thoughtfully, alone or with others.

Take time alone or with others to work through these questions. They build on each other to help you connect this chapter to your own life and experience.

Begin by considering this: name the seven areas of growth from this chapter. Which one can you explain most easily to someone who hasn't read it?

Next, reflect on this: in your own words, explain the difference between independence and interdependence. Why does the balance between them matter for college success?

Take a moment to think about this: think about a recent struggle you faced in college. Which of the seven growth areas does it connect to? How does naming it help you see the struggle differently?

Consider this honestly: compare who you were before college started to who you are now. What parts of your identity have stayed the same? What parts are shifting or changing?

Now ask yourself: look honestly at your current support system—family, friends, mentors, advisors. What's working well? What's missing? Which relationships need more attention from you?

Reflect carefully on this: write a brief purpose statement—two or three sentences about why you're pursuing your education and what you hope to build with your degree.

Finally, consider this: imagine a first-gen student starting college next fall who asks you for advice. What three things would you tell them based on what you've learned so far?

Who you become shows up in what you do every day—how you learn, study, and engage with your education. Chapter 2 explores how you learn best and how to build strategies that actually work for your unique brain.

CHAPTER 2

Understanding Your Unique Wiring

> *"I spent my whole first year feeling like I was doing everything wrong. No one ever explained that college learning was completely different from high school. I had to figure it out the hard way."*
>
> *—First-generation college student*

The way you learn is not a problem to fix. It's a design to understand. Every brain works differently. Some people learn best by reading. Others learn by listening. Others need to do something with their hands before an idea clicks. Some people need total silence to focus. Others actually think better with noise in the background. Some people get ideas quickly.

None of these ways is better or worse. They're just different. And here's the key insight of this chapter: when you understand how your brain actually works, you can build study strategies that fit you instead of fighting against you. You stop trying to force yourself into someone else's mold and start working with your natural strengths.

The student who opens this chapter learned the hard way that college is a different game. What worked before stopped working. That's a common experience, especially for first-gen students who may not have had anyone explain the shift. But the struggle doesn't have to last forever. Once you figure out how you learn best and which strategies actually work, everything gets easier.

In this chapter, we're going to explore how college learning differs from high school, look at what research says actually works for studying, and help you build an approach that matches your unique brain. By the end, you'll have both understanding and practical tools you can use right away.

Let me be clear about something from the start: being a good learner is a skill. It's not something you're born with or without. It's not fixed at birth or determined by your genes. The students who do well in college aren't necessarily smarter than everyone else. They've just figured out how to learn effectively in this new environment. What they've figured out, you can learn too.

The Hidden Rules of College Learning

Before we talk about specific study strategies, we need to name something that often goes unspoken: there's a hidden set of rules in college that nobody explains but everybody is expected to follow. Researchers call this the hidden curriculum. It includes things like unwritten expectations, invisible norms, and ways of doing things that insiders take for granted but outsiders have to discover through trial and error—often painful error.

Students whose parents went to college often absorb these hidden rules without realizing it. They grew up hearing about how college works. They know things like: how to read a syllabus to figure out what really matters, how to talk to a professor without feeling awkward or presumptuous, when to ask for help and how to do it gracefully, what office hours are actually for and that professors want you to come, how to form study groups, what it means when a professor says the reading is 'recommended' versus 'required.'

If you're first-gen, you probably didn't grow up with those dinner table conversations about college. Your parents wanted to help you, but they couldn't teach what they'd never experienced. You're learning the content of your courses and the culture of college at the same time. That's like trying to learn a new sport while also learning the rules of the game—while it's already in progress.

"No one in my family went to college, so I had

to figure everything out on my own. I didn't even know what questions to ask because I didn't know what I didn't know. It felt like everyone else had read a manual I never got."

—First-generation college student

Research by Toutkoushian and colleagues in 2021 showed that first-gen students navigate college differently than students whose parents have degrees. This isn't because first-gen students are less capable or less intelligent. It's because they're essentially doing double duty—learning course material while also learning how college works. That takes more energy and more time. It's exhausting in ways that others don't always see.

Let me make some of these hidden rules visible right now. Professors expect you to do more than just show up and turn in assignments. They expect you to engage with material outside of class on your own. They expect you to think for yourself instead of just memorizing what they say. They expect you to come to office hours even when you're not in crisis—just to talk, ask questions, or discuss ideas. They expect you to take charge of your own learning instead of waiting to be told exactly what to do. These expectations are rarely said out loud because professors assume everyone already knows them. Now you do too.

Part of understanding your unique wiring is recognizing that some of your struggles might not be about your brain at all. They might be about navigating an unfamiliar system without the map that some of your classmates inherited from their families. That's not a personal failing. It's a gap you can close once you see it clearly.

The Big Shift: High School to College

Many students experience the move to college as a shock. The pace is faster. The expectations are higher. The responsibility is greater. The safety net is thinner. In high school, teachers often walked you through material step by step. They reminded you about deadlines. They gave you lots of chances to show what you know. In college, professors expect you to figure things out on your own. They give you a syllabus and assume you'll follow it.

The skills that got you good grades in high school might not work here. That's not because you got dumber over the summer or because you don't belong in college. It's because the game changed and nobody gave you the new playbook. The rules are different, and no one told you.

> *"Time management was my biggest struggle. In high school, the structure was built in. You went to class all day, did homework at night, and the routine carried you. In college, I had all this free time and no idea how to use it. I wasted so much time before I figured out how to manage myself."*
>
> *—First-generation college student*
>
> *"Balancing school and work was much harder than I expected. I kept missing deadlines because I didn't realize how long things would take. A paper I thought would take two hours actually needed six. I had to completely change how I thought about time."*
>
> *—First-generation college student*
>
> *"I thought I was a good student. I had good grades in high school and everyone told me I was smart. Then I got my first college exam back and realized I had no idea what I was doing. The way I had always studied just didn't work anymore. I felt like a fraud."*
>
> *—First-generation college student*

If this sounds like you, take a breath. You're not alone. The gap between high school and college is real, and it catches a lot of students off guard. Many high schools—especially those in lower-income areas where first-gen students often come from —don't have the resources to fully prepare students for college-level work. That's a system problem, not a you problem. It's not your fault that you weren't prepared for something no one prepared you for.

Here's the good news: students figure it out. In my research, students who made it through described an early period of struggle followed by a turning point when things started to click. Sometimes this happened in the second semester. Sometimes not until the second year. But it happened. The skills for college success can be built. It just takes time and the right approach—and the willingness to try new things.

> *"What kept me going was figuring out how to manage my time and actually seeing progress in my work. It took a while—most of my first year was rough—but things eventually started to make sense. Once I found strategies that worked for my brain, everything changed."*
>
> *—First-generation college student*

Notice what this student said: strategies that worked for my brain. That's the key. There's no one-size-fits-all approach to studying. You need to find what works for you specifically. That starts with understanding how learning actually happens.

Thinking About Your Thinking

One of the most powerful skills you can build as a learner has a fancy name: metacognition. It just means thinking about your own thinking. It's being aware of how you learn, what strategies you use, and whether those strategies are actually working or just making you feel busy.

Students with strong metacognition know the difference between really understanding something and just being familiar with it. That's a crucial difference we'll explore more later. They can tell when a study strategy is working and when it's not producing real results. They can figure out why they're struggling and adjust their approach. They don't just study harder when things aren't working. They study differently.

Metacognition has three parts that work together in a cycle. Before you study, you plan. You ask yourself: What am I trying to learn today? What strategy will I use, and why? How long will I study? What distractions do I need to remove? This kind of planning sets you up for success instead of just hoping things work out.

During study, you monitor. You check in with yourself regularly: Am I actually understanding this, or am I just looking at words on a page? Could I explain this to someone else in my own words? Is my strategy working, or should I try something different? Am I actually focused, or has my mind drifted somewhere else? This kind of checking keeps you from wasting time on approaches that aren't producing results.

After study, you evaluate. You reflect honestly: What worked today? What didn't? What would I do differently next time? How well do I really know this material if I'm being honest with myself? This kind of reflection builds knowledge about yourself as a learner that you can use in the future.

These questions might feel awkward at first. You might not be used to watching your own mind this closely. But with practice, it becomes more natural. You train yourself to be an active participant in your learning instead of just going through the motions on autopilot.

Research consistently shows that students with strong metacognitive skills do better than those without them, even when you account for differences in natural ability or prior preparation. In other words, learning how to learn might be more important than being naturally smart. And the good news is that metacognition is a skill you can develop through deliberate practice.

What Actually Works: Study Strategies That Stick

Here's something that might surprise you: many of the most common study strategies don't work very well. Reading your textbook over and over. Highlighting important passages until the page is bright yellow. Copying your notes again and again. These are popular because they're easy and they feel productive. But research shows they often fail to create lasting learning.

Why do these strategies stick around if they don't work? Because they create an illusion of learning. When you reread something, it feels familiar. That familiarity feels like understanding. When you highlight key points, you feel like you're engaging with the material. You're doing something. But feeling like you know something is different from actually knowing it when it counts.

Research on learning has found several strategies that actually work. They share something in common: they require effort. Learning that feels easy often doesn't stick. Learning that involves struggle—the right kind of struggle, not helpless frustration—builds knowledge that lasts. Let me walk you through the strategies with the strongest research support.

The first strategy is testing yourself. Instead of just reviewing your notes, close them and try to remember what you learned. Use flashcards to quiz yourself. Take practice tests. Explain ideas out loud without looking at the material. Write down everything you can remember about a topic, then check what you missed. This is called retrieval practice, and it's one of the most powerful learning tools we know about.

Why does testing yourself work so well? Because the effort of trying to remember something strengthens your memory far more than just looking at it again. Every time you successfully pull something from memory, you make it easier to remember next time. The path gets stronger each time you walk it. And when you fail to remember something, you learn exactly what you need to work on. The failure is useful information.

Many students avoid testing themselves because it feels harder than rereading. You sit there struggling to remember, feeling unsure of yourself, when you could just open your notes and have the answer right in front of you. That's more comfortable. But that struggle is the point. The effort of trying to remember is what makes memories stick. Easy practice creates weak memories. Effortful practice creates strong ones.

The second strategy is spacing out your study. Studying a little bit over many days works much better than cramming everything into one long session. Five two-hour sessions spread across a week produce more learning than one ten-hour marathon the night before the exam. This is called the spacing effect, and it's one of the most reliable findings in all of learning research.

Cramming feels efficient because you cover a lot of material quickly and it's fresh in your mind for the test. But crammed information fades fast after the exam is over. You might pass the test, but you won't remember the material for future classes that build on it. Spaced study builds knowledge that lasts weeks, months, and years.

The third strategy is connecting new information to what you already know. Ask yourself questions as you study: How does this relate to other things I've learned? Why does this make sense? What examples can I think of from my own life? How would I explain this to someone who's never heard of it? This is called elaboration, and it works because learning is fundamentally about building connections.

Information that links to things you already know has multiple paths for you to reach it. If you can't remember it one way, you can access it through its connections. Information that sits alone in your mind, not connected to anything else, is easy to lose because there's only one fragile path to reach it.

The fourth strategy is mixing up what you study. Instead of focusing on one topic until you master it, then moving to the next, try switching between different topics or types of problems in the same session. This is called interleaving. It feels harder and slower in the moment, but it produces better long-term results. It forces your brain to keep retrieving different information and figuring out which approach to use for each problem.

Research by Collings and Eaton in 2021 found that even where you study matters. Students who created consistent, structured study environments did better in their first year and were more likely to come back for their second year. The practical lesson: your environment affects your learning more than you might think. Set yourself up for success by creating a space that helps you focus.

The Trap of Fake Learning

Understanding fake learning is crucial for becoming a successful student. Fake learning happens when you feel like you're learning but you're actually not. It's when you feel like you know something that you can't actually use or remember when it counts—on the exam, in a future class, or in real life.

The trap comes from confusing familiarity with true understanding. When you read something again, it feels familiar. You recognize the words. The examples make sense as you read them. You think, 'I get this. I know this.' But what you really mean is, 'This looks familiar right now while I'm looking at it.'

Familiarity in the moment is different from being able to recall and use knowledge later when the book is closed. You might recognize the right answer when you see it on a multiple-choice test. But could you produce that answer from scratch on an essay exam? You might follow along when a professor explains a concept in class. But could you explain it yourself to someone else?

The strategies that actually work—testing yourself, spacing your study, making connections, mixing topics—often feel harder than rereading and highlighting. You might feel like you're learning less because the process is more difficult and more uncomfortable. But that feeling is misleading. The difficulty is a sign that real learning is happening. Easy studying produces weak knowledge. Effortful studying produces strong knowledge that sticks.

To beat fake learning, you need to test yourself honestly. Don't ask, 'Does this feel familiar?' Ask, 'Can I actually recall this without looking at my notes? Can I explain this in my own words to someone else? Can I apply this to a problem I've never seen before?' If the answer is no, you haven't really learned it yet, no matter how familiar it feels when you're looking at it.

Finding What Works for You

While research has found strategies that work for most people, there's still real variation in how different individuals learn best. Part of understanding your unique wiring is figuring out what works specifically for you, not just what works on average.

Think about some questions. When do you learn best? Some people are sharpest in the morning. Others hit their stride at night. Your peak focus time is when you should do your hardest thinking work. What environment helps you focus? Some people need total silence. Others actually work better with background noise or music. Some need a specific study spot. Others can focus anywhere. There's no right answer—just your answer.

Be careful about the popular idea of learning styles—the notion that people are visual learners or auditory learners and need to receive information in their preferred way to learn well. Research hasn't supported this idea the way it's usually presented. Most people learn best when they engage with material in multiple ways—reading, listening, discussing, writing, doing—rather than sticking to just one approach.

What does vary meaningfully between people is things like: when you study, where you study, what conditions help you focus, how you structure your time, how often you need breaks. Try different approaches and pay close attention to results. Let evidence guide you, not just comfort or habit. Be willing to try strategies that feel uncomfortable at first if the research says they work.

Keep a study journal for a few weeks. Track what strategies you use, how long you study, where you study, and what results you see on exams and papers. Look for patterns. You might discover that you do your best work in the morning at the library. Or that you need breaks every forty-five minutes. Or that you learn better when you study with others than when you study alone. This self-knowledge is valuable and will serve you for years.

Getting Help: Using Campus Resources

Your campus has resources designed to support your learning—tutoring centers, writing centers, academic coaching, study groups, professor office hours, peer mentoring, and more. These services exist because research shows they work. Colleges invest in them because they help students succeed. But they only help if you actually use them.

Many students—especially first-gen students—don't use these resources as much as they could. Sometimes they don't know the resources exist. Sometimes they're not sure if they're allowed to use them or who they're meant for. Sometimes they worry about what it might mean about them if they need help. They fear that seeking help is an admission that they don't belong.

> *"I didn't use tutoring at first because I didn't know where to start. I thought it might be only for*

athletes or students in real trouble. I didn't realize it was for everyone who wanted to do better."

—First-generation college student

"I was embarrassed to go to the writing center because I thought it meant I was a bad writer. Then I learned that even the best students use it regularly. It's not about being bad. It's about getting feedback to improve."

—First-generation college student

"The writing center became my second home. Without it, I don't think I would have made it through my first year. The tutors didn't just fix my papers—they taught me how to think about writing in a completely different way."

—First-generation college student

Notice the contrast in these experiences. First came hesitation and embarrassment. Then came the discovery that help was available and useful and nothing to be ashamed of. This pattern is common. Many first-gen students hold back from seeking help because of the hidden curriculum—they don't realize these resources are meant for them too.

Research by Delmas and Childs in 2021 showed that early alert systems—where professors or advisors reach out when they notice a student struggling—help connect students with support before small problems become big crises. If someone from your college reaches out to you, that's not a judgment or a criticism. It's an invitation to use resources that can help you succeed.

Let me be direct: if you're not using available support services, you're leaving valuable tools on the table. Find out what your campus offers. Visit the tutoring center even if you're not failing a class. Go to professor office hours even if you don't have a specific question—just introduce yourself. Use the writing center for every major paper, not just the ones you're struggling with. These are strategies of successful students, not signs of weakness or not belonging.

The Stress-Study Connection

My research found a clear pattern: academic stress and study habits affect each other in a cycle that can go in either direction. Students who felt more stressed tended to have weaker study habits. And weaker habits led to results that increased stress —bad grades, missed deadlines, falling behind, feeling overwhelmed. This negative cycle can feel impossible to escape once you're caught in it.

But the good news is that the cycle can also run the other direction. Students who built better study strategies said their stress went down over time. Seeing progress built confidence. Confidence made it easier to maintain good habits. Good habits produced better results. Better results reduced stress further. Success fed more success in an upward spiral.

> *"Once I got my study routine figured out, everything else got easier. I was less stressed because I knew what I needed to do and when I was going to do it. Before that, everything felt chaotic and out of control. Having a system gave me back a sense of control over my life."*
>
> *—First-generation college student*

If you're stuck in the negative cycle right now, don't try to fix everything at once. That's overwhelming and usually fails within a few days. Start with one small change that you can actually stick with. Maybe it's a consistent study time each day. Maybe it's a weekly planning session on Sunday evening. Maybe it's regular visits to a campus resource. Small improvements add up over time into big changes. One good habit leads to another.

Managing Your Time

Time management came up constantly in my research. Students mentioned it more than almost anything else as a challenge. First-gen students often juggle more responsibilities than their peers: significant work hours, family obligations, commuting, money pressures that demand attention. There's simply less time available for studying, which means the time you do have must be used wisely.

Good time management isn't about finding more hours in the day. There are only twenty-four, and you can't change that no matter how hard you wish. It's about using the hours you have more intentionally. Here's what that looks like in practice.

First, know where your time actually goes. For one week, track how you spend every hour. Not how you think you spend it or how you wish you spent it, but how you actually spend it. Most people are surprised by what they find. Time you thought was productive might be filled with distraction. Small pockets of wasted time might add up to hours when you count them all.

Second, put first things first. Not everything deserves equal attention. Figure out your most important tasks—the ones that will have the biggest impact on your success—and protect time for them. Learn to say no to things that don't serve your goals, even when saying no feels uncomfortable. This is especially important for first-gen students who may face extra demands from family who don't fully understand how much college requires.

Third, use a planning system consistently. A paper planner, a phone app, a simple notebook—it doesn't matter what you use as long as you use it every day. When you trust your system to remember things, your brain is freed up for actual learning. Write down assignments, deadlines, and commitments. Check your system daily and weekly.

Fourth, build in cushion. Things always take longer than you expect. Problems always come up that you didn't anticipate. Plan for this reality by starting things early and leaving room for the unexpected. If nothing goes wrong, you'll finish ahead of schedule and feel great. If something does go wrong, you'll have room to handle it without a crisis.

Fifth, match your tasks to your energy. Everyone has times of day when they're more alert and times when they're less so. Do your hardest thinking during your peak hours. Save routine tasks for when your energy naturally dips. Don't waste your best brain time on email or social media.

> *"I used to think I didn't have enough time to study. Then I tracked my time for a week and found hours I was wasting without realizing it. The time was there all along. I just wasn't using it well."*
>
> *—First-generation college student*

Building Your Learning System

Putting all of this together, I want you to think about building a learning system—a set of regular practices and routines that support your success over time. A system is more reliable than motivation because it works even on days when you don't feel like studying. A system builds momentum because each good day reinforces the next. A system frees up mental energy because you don't have to decide what to do each time—the system already has the answer.

Your learning system should include several key parts, adjusted to fit your actual life. First, regular study times and places. When you study at the same time in the same place, your brain learns to shift into focus mode automatically. You spend less energy getting started because your brain knows what's coming.

Second, weekly planning time. Even thirty minutes on Sunday evening can prevent chaos all week. Look at what's coming up. Schedule your study time specifically. Identify potential problems before they hit you by surprise.

Third, effective study strategies built into your routine. Testing yourself. Spacing your study. Making connections. Mixing topics. Don't wait to decide whether to use these strategies each time you sit down. Make them automatic parts of how you always study.

Fourth, regular use of support services. Make office hours, tutoring, and the writing center part of your normal routine, not just emergency responses when you're already in trouble. Schedule them like you schedule classes.

Fifth, time for reflection. Build in moments to think about what's working and what's not. Maybe at the end of each week, take ten minutes to review: What went well? What didn't? What will I do differently next week? Adjust your system based on evidence, not just feelings.

Your system will be unique to you. It needs to account for your class schedule, your work obligations, your family responsibilities, your energy patterns, and your specific challenges. It needs to be realistic—something you can sustain over months, not just during exam week. And it needs to be flexible enough to adjust when life changes.

Don't try to build a perfect system overnight. That's a recipe for failure. Start with one piece. Build that habit until it's automatic—which usually takes a few weeks of consistency. Then add another piece. Over time, your system will become stronger and more effective, and you'll have to think about it less and less.

> *"I finally realized that success in college isn't about being smart. It's about having systems. The students who do well have figured out how to organize their time and their studying. Once I built my own system, everything got easier."*
>
> *—First-generation college student*

What Research Helps Us Understand

Research on learning shows that effective strategies require effort and often feel harder than passive approaches like rereading. Strategies like testing yourself, spacing your study, making connections, and mixing topics build lasting knowledge that can be recalled and used later. Students who use campus support services and develop awareness of their own learning show stronger outcomes. The connection between stress and study habits runs both ways: better habits lead to lower stress, which makes it easier to maintain good habits. First-gen students who build systematic approaches to learning show persistence rates similar to their peers whose parents went to college. Understanding how you learn best is a skill that develops through deliberate attention and practice.

The Huddle

Take time to reflect on these questions thoughtfully, alone or with others.

Take time alone or with others to work through these questions. They build on each other to help you connect this chapter to your own learning life.

Begin by considering this: list the four main study strategies from this chapter that research shows actually work. Which one is newest to you?

Next, reflect on this: explain in your own words why testing yourself works better than rereading. What's happening in your brain that makes retrieval practice so powerful?

Take a moment to think about this: think about how you studied for your last major exam. Which strategies from this chapter did you use? Which ones did you skip? What would you do differently next time?

Consider this honestly: track your time for three days this

week. Where does your time actually go? What patterns do you notice? Where are you losing time without realizing it?

Now ask yourself: look at the campus resources available to you—tutoring, writing center, office hours, advising. Which ones are you using well? Which ones have you been avoiding, and why?

Reflect carefully on this: design a weekly learning system for yourself. Include when and where you'll study, what strategies you'll use, and which support services you'll build into your routine.

Finally, consider this: write a brief letter to your future self for the week before finals. What advice would you give based on what you've learned in this chapter?

Understanding how you learn is essential—but knowledge without action fades quickly. Chapter 3 explores how to build habits that turn good intentions into lasting change.

CHAPTER 3

Building Habits That Sustain Success

"The turning point for me was when I stopped trying to rely on willpower and started building routines. Once certain things became automatic, I had energy left over for the hard stuff."

—First-generation college student

Motivation is a liar. It shows up strong on the first day of the semester, full of promises. You're going to study every day. You're going to stay on top of your reading. You're going to use all those strategies from the last chapter. And for a few days, maybe even a couple weeks, motivation delivers. Then it disappears. You're tired. You're stressed. You don't feel like it. And suddenly all those good intentions evaporate like morning fog.

If you've ever started strong and then faded, you're not alone. That's not a character flaw. That's how motivation works for almost everyone. It's unreliable. It comes and goes based on your mood, your energy, your stress level, whether you slept well, what else is happening in your life. Relying on motivation to carry you through college is like relying on the weather to always be sunny. It's a setup for disappointment.

The student who opens this chapter discovered something important: the solution isn't more willpower. It's better systems. When you build the right habits, you don't have to decide each day whether to do the right thing. You just do it automatically, the way you brush your teeth without having an internal debate about it every morning. Habits save your limited willpower for the moments when you really need it.

This chapter is about how to build habits that stick—the kind that carry you through the semester even when motivation takes a vacation. We'll look at how habits actually work in your brain, why some attempts to change fail while others succeed, and how to set yourself up so that good behaviors become automatic. By the end, you'll have a practical toolkit for turning your good intentions into lasting change.

Here's the key insight: successful students aren't people with superhuman willpower. They're people who have built systems that don't require superhuman willpower. They've made the right choices easy and the wrong choices hard. They've designed their environment and their routines to support their goals. You can do the same thing. It's not about being a different kind of person. It's about setting things up so that success becomes the default.

The Problem with Willpower

Most people think of willpower like a muscle—the more you use it, the stronger it gets. But research shows something different. Willpower is more like a battery. You start the day with a full charge, and every decision you make drains it a little. By the end of a long, stressful day, the battery is low. That's when the pizza sounds better than the salad. That's when Netflix wins over studying. That's when you skip the workout you planned.

This is called decision fatigue, and it affects everyone regardless of how disciplined they think they are. The more choices you make throughout the day—even small ones that seem trivial—the less energy you have for making good choices later. That's why you might have great intentions in the morning but find yourself making poor decisions by evening. Your willpower battery ran out before the day did.

For college students, this is a big deal. Your days are full of decisions. What to eat. What to wear. Which assignment to work on first. Whether to go to that optional study session. Whether to respond to that text right now or later. How long to scroll through social media. Each little choice takes a small bite out of your willpower reserves. By dinner time, you've made hundreds of small decisions, and the tank is running low.

First-gen students often face even more decision fatigue than their peers. You might be making decisions about things that other students don't have to think about—navigating financial aid on your own, figuring out how to balance work and school, managing family expectations, learning the hidden rules of college that others absorbed automatically at home. All of that takes mental energy that you then don't have for academic decisions.

> *"I used to wonder why I could never stick with my study plans. I'd start strong every semester and then fall apart after a few weeks. I thought something was wrong with me—like I just didn't have what it takes. Now I realize I was trying to do everything through willpower, and that's not sustainable for anyone."*
>
> *—First-generation college student*

The solution isn't to develop superhuman willpower. That's a losing game because willpower has real limits. The solution is to reduce how much willpower you need in the first place. That's where habits come in. When something becomes a habit, you do it without having to decide. It happens automatically. It doesn't drain your battery. You save your limited willpower for the moments that truly require unexpected problems, the real decisions, the things that can't be automated.

Think about brushing your teeth. You probably don't have an internal debate each morning about whether to do it. You don't weigh the pros and cons. You don't need motivation or willpower. You just do it because it's a habit—it's what you do in the morning, period. Imagine if more of your successful student behaviors were like that. Imagine if studying at a certain time, or reviewing your notes, or going to office hours happened just as automatically. That's the power of habits. They take things off your decision plate entirely.

How Habits Actually Work

To build better habits, it helps to understand how they work in your brain. Every habit has three parts that form a loop: a cue, a routine, and a reward. The cue is the trigger that tells your brain to start the automatic behavior. The routine is the behavior itself—what you actually do. The reward is the benefit you get, which tells your brain this loop is worth remembering and repeating.

Here's a simple example. You sit down at your desk after dinner (cue). You open your textbook and study for an hour (routine). You feel good about making progress and check something off your list (reward). If you repeat this enough times, your brain starts to connect sitting at your desk after dinner with studying. Eventually, it becomes automatic. The cue triggers the routine without you having to think about it or argue with yourself.

The problem is that this same loop works for bad habits too. You feel stressed (cue). You open social media and scroll (routine). You get a temporary escape from the stress (reward). Do this enough times, and stress automatically triggers scrolling. You don't even decide to do it—your brain just runs the program before you consciously realize what's happening.

Understanding this loop gives you power over your habits. You can change any part of it. You can modify the cue—what triggers the behavior. You can substitute a different routine—a better behavior in response to the same trigger. You can adjust to making good habits more satisfying and bad habits less appealing. The loop is the mechanism, and once you understand it, you can work with it instead of being controlled by it.

Most people try to change habits through pure willpower: I'll just stop doing that or I'll just start doing this. But that approach fights against how your brain actually works. It's much more effective to work with the habit loop instead of against it. Design your cues deliberately, plan your routines specifically, and set up rewards that reinforce what you want to do.

> *"I never understood why I kept checking my phone while studying until I realized it was a habit loop. I'd feel stuck on a problem—that was my cue. I'd grab my phone—that was my routine. I'd get a little bit of entertainment—that was my reward. Once I saw the pattern, I could start changing it. I put my phone in another room so the cue couldn't trigger the routine."*
>
> *—First-generation college student*

The Power of Starting Small

When people try to build new habits, they usually start too big. They want to study three hours every day. They want to exercise five times a week. They want to completely overhaul their eating, sleeping, and social media use all at once. This feels good in the planning stage—bold and ambitious, like you're really going to change this time. But it almost always fails.

The problem with big changes is that they require too much willpower to maintain. For the first few days, your motivation is high enough to power through. But as soon as life gets stressful or you have a bad day or you're tired or you're dealing with something unexpected, the whole thing collapses. Then you feel like a failure, which makes it even harder to try again. You've not only failed at the habit—you've collected more evidence that you can't change.

The research on habit formation points to a different approach: start so small it feels almost silly. Instead of studying for three hours, commit to studying for five minutes. Instead of going to the gym every day, commit to putting on your workout clothes. Instead of reading a chapter, commit to reading one page. Make the habit so easy that you can't say no, even on your worst day.

This might seem pointless. What good is five minutes of studying? But here's what happens: once you start, you usually keep going. The hardest part of most tasks is beginning. If you can get yourself to start, momentum takes over. And even if you really do only study for five minutes, you've done something crucial—you've kept the habit alive. You've reinforced the pattern in your brain. Tomorrow it will be a little easier to do it again.

Research by Klussman and colleagues in 2021 found that students who felt truly connected to their goals—not just going through the motions—showed stronger motivation and better attitudes toward school. But that connection often builds through small, consistent actions rather than dramatic overhauls. Small wins create confidence. Confidence strengthens commitment. Commitment leads to bigger wins over time. It's a positive spiral, but it starts with tiny steps.

> *"I tried so many times to become a morning person who studied before class. I'd set my alarm early, and I'd do it for maybe three days before giving up and hitting snooze. Then I tried something different—I just committed to reviewing my flashcards for two minutes with my morning coffee. That was it. Two minutes. But I actually did it every day, and eventually those two minutes became twenty, then forty. Small steps actually worked when big leaps always failed."*
>
> *—First-generation college student*

The key is to focus on consistency over intensity. It's better to study for thirty minutes every day than to study for five hours once a week. It's better to do a small thing reliably than a big thing occasionally. Habits are built through repetition, and you can only repeat what you can actually sustain. A tiny habit you do every day beats an ambitious habit you do once and then abandon.

Designing Your Environment

One of the most powerful ways to build good habits is to change your environment. Your surroundings constantly send you cues that trigger behaviors, often without you realizing it. If your phone is on your desk while you study, it cues you to check it. If junk food is visible in your room, it cues you to eat it. If your textbook is buried under a pile of stuff, it cues you to ignore it. Your environment is always talking to you, shaping your behavior in ways both obvious and subtle.

The good news is that you can redesign your environment to send better cues. Make good behaviors easy and obvious. Make bad behaviors hard and hidden. This is called choice architecture, and it's one of the most effective behavior change strategies we know about. The idea is simple: instead of relying on willpower to make good choices, set up your environment so that good choices are the easy choices.

Here's what this looks like in practice. If you want to study more, set up a dedicated study space where studying is the only thing that happens. Keep your textbook and notes visible and ready to use. If you want to check your phone less, put it in another room while you work—not just face down on your desk, but actually out of sight and out of reach. Make the good choice easy and the bad choice inconvenient.

Research by Collings and Eaton in 2021 showed that students who created structured study environments had better first-year grades and were more likely to return for their second year. Where and how you set up your space matters more than you might think. Your environment is constantly shaping your behavior, whether you notice it or not. You can either let that happen by accident or take control of it deliberately.

> *"I rearranged my whole room to make studying easier. I got my textbooks out of my backpack and put them on my desk where I could see them. I started charging my phone in the kitchen instead of my bedroom. I put my planner right next to my bed, so I saw it first thing in the morning. These little changes made a huge difference. I didn't have to rely on willpower because my environment was doing the work for me."*
>
> *—First-generation college student*

Think about the behaviors you want to increase and decrease. For each one, ask: How can I change my environment to make this easier or harder? Sometimes small changes have big effects. Moving your phone charger to another room takes two minutes but can save hours of distraction over a semester. Putting your textbook on your pillow means you have to move it before you can go to sleep—and you might as well read a page while you're at it.

Your social environment matters too. The people around you shape your habits powerfully. If your friends study regularly, you're more likely to study. If your roommate stays up late playing video games, you're more likely to do the same. We tend to adopt the behaviors of the people we spend time with. You don't have to abandon your friends but be aware of how your social environment influences you. Seek out study partners. Join groups where the norm is success. Build relationships that support your goals rather than undermining them.

Habit Stacking: Building on What You Already Do

One of the easiest ways to build a new habit is to attach it to something you already do automatically. This is called habit stacking. The formula is simple: After I do [current habit], I will do [new habit]. You're using an existing routine as a cue for a new behavior.

For example: After I pour my morning coffee, I will review my planner for the day. After I sit down on the bus, I will read for ten minutes. After I finish dinner, I will study for one hour. After I brush my teeth at night, I will write down three things I learned today. The existing habit becomes the trigger for the new one. You're piggybacking on something that's already automatic.

This works because you're not trying to remember to do something at a vague time. You're linking it to something you already do without thinking. The current habit serves as a reliable cue. You don't have to set reminders or rely on motivation to kick in at the right moment. The sequence happens naturally because one thing leads directly to the next.

When building a habit stack, be specific about the when and where. Vague intentions like 'I'll study more' don't become habits because they don't have a clear trigger. Specific plans like 'After I get home from my Tuesday class, I'll study in the library for one hour before going to my room' have a much better chance of sticking. The more specific your plan is, the more likely you are to follow through because there's no ambiguity about when the habit should happen.

> *"I could never remember to check my syllabi for upcoming deadlines until I stacked it with something I already did. Now, every Sunday when I sit down for dinner, I spend five minutes looking at what's due that week. It's just part of my Sunday routine now. I don't even think about it—it just happens automatically."*
>
> *—First-generation college student*

Think about your current daily routines. What do you already do reliably, without thinking? Those are perfect anchor points for new habits. Attach a small new behavior to each anchor, and you can build a whole chain of positive habits without needing to remember each one separately. The chain carries itself once you set it up.

When You Fall Off: Dealing with Setbacks

Here's something important to understand you will have setbacks. You will miss days. You will fall back into old patterns sometimes. This is not a sign that you've failed or that habit-building doesn't work for you. It's just part of the process for everyone, including the most successful people you know.

The difference between people who build lasting habits and people who don't isn't that the successful ones never slip up. It's how they respond when they do slip up. People who fail at habits tend to see a setback as proof that they can't change. They miss one day and think, 'See, I knew I couldn't do this.' Then they give up entirely. This is called the what-the-hell effect—once you've broken your streak, you figure you might as well keep going in the wrong direction.

People who succeed at habits see setbacks differently. They miss one day and think, 'Okay, that happened. How do I get back on track tomorrow?' They don't let one slip become a slide. They have a rule: never miss twice. Missing once is a mistake. Missing twice is the start of a new (bad) habit. The goal isn't perfect; the goal is quick recovery.

Research by Rehr and colleagues in 2021 found that students who developed strong coping strategies were more likely to persist through challenges. Building habits is part of resilience, but so is bouncing back when habits break down. The most resilient students aren't those who never stumble. They're the ones who know how to get up quickly.

> *"I used to be so hard on myself when I missed a day. If I skipped my morning study session, I'd feel like a failure and then skip the rest of the week too. Now I have a different rule: just get*

> *back to it the next day. No guilt, no drama. Just start again. That simple change made my habits so much more sustainable."*
>
> *—First-generation college student*

When you do have a setback, get curious instead of critical. Ask yourself: What happened? What got in the way? Was my plan realistic? What can I adjust so it works better next time? Treat it as information, not as judgment. Each setback teaches you something about what you need to succeed. The information is valuable if you're willing to learn from it.

Also, be careful about all-or-nothing thinking. Some progress is always better than no progress. If you plan to study for an hour but only have twenty minutes, do twenty minutes. If you plan to go to the gym but only have energy for a walk, take a walk. Doing a reduced version of your habit keeps the pattern alive and is infinitely better than doing nothing. Something beats nothing every time.

Becoming a Different Kind of Person

The most powerful habit changes happen at the level of identity. Instead of focusing on what you want to achieve (outcomes) or what you want to do (behaviors), focus on who you want to become (identity). When your habits become part of how you see yourself, they stick much more powerfully than when they're just things you're trying to do.

Here's the difference. Outcome-based thinking says: 'I want to get good grades.' Behavior-based thinking says: 'I want to study every day.' Identity-based thinking says: 'I am a serious student.' When studying becomes part of who you are—not just something you do—it feels natural and automatic. You study because that's what serious students do, and you're a serious student. There's no internal debate.

Every action you take is a vote for the type of person you

want to become. Each time you study when you don't feel like it, you're casting a vote for being a disciplined person. Each time you ask for help, you're casting a vote to be a resourceful person. Each time you show up for yourself, you're casting a vote for being someone who follows through. No single vote is decisive, but over time they add up to an identity.

Research by Museus and Chang in 2021 found that students with a strong sense of who they are show more resilience when facing challenges. Your identity becomes an anchor. When you see yourself as someone who persists, you persist even when it's hard. When you see yourself as a learner, you embrace challenges as opportunities to grow rather than threats to avoid.

> *"The biggest shift for me was when I stopped saying 'I'm trying to be a good student' and started saying 'I am a good student.' It sounds small, but it changed everything. Good students do their reading, so I did my reading. Good students go to office hours, so I went to office hours. I was living up to an identity instead of fighting against myself."*
>
> *—First-generation college student*

Start to pay attention to the story you tell yourself about who you are. Do you say, 'I'm not a morning person' or 'I'm bad at math' or 'I'm just not organized'? Those identity statements become self-fulfilling. You act in ways that confirm the story because you believe it's true. But you can change the story. You can start telling yourself a different one and then taking actions that support it.

You don't have to believe the new story completely at first. That's okay. Act as if it's true and let the evidence accumulate. Each time you act like the person you want to become, you collect another piece of evidence. Eventually, the new identity feels natural because you've proven it to yourself through action. The belief follows the behavior.

Systems Beat Goals

Goals are useful for setting direction, but systems are what actually produce results. A goal is the outcome you want—get an A in biology, make the dean's list, graduate with honors. A system is what you do regularly to move toward that outcome—your daily study routine, your weekly review session, your monthly check-in with your advisor.

Here's the problem with focusing too much on goals: you're in a constant state of not having achieved them yet. You only feel successful when you finally cross the finish line. But if you focus on your system—on showing up every day and doing what your system says—you can feel successful every time you follow through. You're winning every day, not waiting to win someday.

Goals also create an odd situation where achieving them can actually hurt you. People who focus only on goals sometimes let their habits slide once they hit their target. They get the grade they wanted and then stop doing what got them there. But people who focus on systems keep going because the system is the point. They're not done when they achieve a goal; they're done when they stop being the kind of person who follows their system.

Research by Bennett and colleagues in 2022 emphasized that student success isn't just about individual effort—it's about having structures that support sustained engagement. Your personal system is the structure that supports you when motivation fades and life gets complicated. It's the thing that keeps working even when everything else is falling apart.

> *"I used to set goals for each semester and then wonder why I never hit them. The problem was I only had goals—I didn't have systems. Now I focus on what I do every day and every week. I have my routines, my study times, my check-ins.*

The goals take care of themselves when the system is solid."

—First-generation college student

Think about it this way: if you completely ignored your goals and just focused on your system, would you still get good results? If you have a good system for studying, attending class, getting help when you need it, and managing your time, you'll probably do well even without thinking about specific grade targets. The system produces the outcomes automatically.

So spend less energy worrying about goals and more energy designing and following your system. What will you do every day? Every week? What routines will you follow? What habits will you build? Those are the questions that matter. The goals will follow.

Making Your Habits Stick for Good

Building a habit takes time. Research suggests it takes an average of about two months for a new behavior to become automatic, though this varies widely depending on the person and the behavior. Some simple habits might stick in a few weeks. More complex ones might take several months. Be patient with yourself. You're rewiring your brain, and that doesn't happen overnight.

Here are some principles that help habits stick over the long term. First, make it obvious—use clear cues that trigger your habit. Put your running shoes by the door. Set your textbook on your pillow. Use visual reminders of what you want to do. The more visible the cue, the more likely you are to respond to it.

Second, make it attractive—pair habits you need to do with things you enjoy. Listen to your favorite music only while studying. Reward yourself with something you like after completing a difficult task. Find ways to make the habit feel good, not just useful. Your brain needs to associate the habit with positive feelings.

Third, make it easy—reduce friction for good habits and add friction for bad ones. Prepare your study space in advance so everything is ready when you sit down. Remove distractions before they tempt you. Make the default choice the good choice by setting up your environment to support it.

Fourth, make it satisfying. Reward yourself instantly. Track your progress visually so you can see your streak growing. Celebrate small wins. Give yourself credit for showing up. Your brain needs positive feedback to reinforce the behavior, and that feedback needs to come quickly.

Fifth, be consistent with your timing. Habits form faster when they're tied to a specific time and place. 'I'll study after dinner at my desk' becomes a habit faster than 'I'll study when I have time.' The more consistent the cue, the stronger the habit becomes over time.

> *"What finally made my habits stick was making them visible. I got a big wall calendar and put an X on every day I followed my study routine. After a few weeks, I had this chain of X's, and I didn't want to break it. Seeing my progress made me want to keep going."*
>
> *—First-generation college student*

Remember that building habits is a skill, and like any skill, you get better at it with practice. The first habit you try to build might be hard. But each time you successfully build a habit, you learn something about how your brain works and what strategies help you. Over time, you become someone who knows how to change your own behavior. That's an incredibly valuable skill for the rest of your life, far beyond college.

What Research Helps Us Understand

Research on habit formation shows that lasting change comes not from willpower but from well-designed systems and environments. Habits form through a loop of cue, routine, and reward that becomes automatic with repetition. Starting small, stacking new habits onto existing ones, and designing supportive environments all increase the likelihood that habits will stick. Students who build identity-based habits—seeing themselves as the kind of person who does the behavior—show more persistence than those focused only on outcomes. Consistency matters more than intensity: regular small actions produce better results than occasional big efforts. When setbacks occur, the key is getting back on track quickly rather than giving up entirely.

The Huddle

Take time to reflect on these questions thoughtfully, alone or with others.

Reflect on these questions solo or with others; they help you build lasting habits.

Begin by considering this: describe the three parts of a habit loop. Give an example of a good habit and a bad habit, showing how each part works.

Next, reflect on this: explain in your own words why starting small is more effective than starting big when building new habits. What makes tiny changes more sustainable?

Take a moment to think about this: choose one habit you want to build this semester. Design a habit stack: After I do [existing habit], I will do [new habit]. Be specific about time and place.

Take a look at your surroundings—your room, study area, phone. Which cues prompt positive habits? Which lead to negative ones? What can you change?

Now ask yourself: think about a habit you've tried to build in the past that didn't stick. What went wrong? Using what you've learned in this chapter, what would you do differently now?

Reflect carefully on this: write an identity statement for the student you want to become. Start with 'I am...' Then list three specific habits that person would have.

Finally, consider this: design a complete system for one area of your college life (studying, health, time management). Include daily routines, weekly practices, environmental changes, and how you'll track progress.

Good habits create a foundation, but college success also requires connection. Chapter 4 explores how to build the relationships and support networks that help you thrive.

CHAPTER 4

Building Relationships That Support Your Success

Building Connections That Sustain You

> *"The relationships I built in college saved me. There were times I wanted to quit, and it was the people around me—my mentor, my study group, even a professor who noticed I was struggling—who helped me find a reason to stay."*
>
> *—First-generation college student*

College is not a solo sport. You might think success is all about your effort, your discipline, your intelligence. But the research tells a different story. The students who make it through, especially first-gen students, almost always point to relationships as a key reason they stayed. Someone believed in them. Someone showed them the way. Someone was there when things got hard.

The student who opens this chapter names this directly: relationships saved her. That's not an exaggeration or a nice thing to say. Study after study confirms that feeling connected—to mentors, to peers, to the institution itself—is one of the strongest predictors of whether students persist in graduation. You can have all the study skills in the world, but if you feel alone and disconnected, the odds of making it drop dramatically.

This chapter is about building the relationships that will sustain you through college. We'll look at different types of connections you need, how to build them even when it feels awkward or scary, and how to maintain your important relationships back home while growing new ones at school. Finally, you'll have a clearer picture of the support network you need and practical strategies for building it.

Here's something important to understand right from the start: asking for help and building relationships isn't a sign of weakness. It's actually a sign of wisdom and strength. The most successful people in any field know that no one makes it alone. They build teams around them. They find mentors who guide them. They cultivate networks of support. You're not supposed to do this by yourself. That's not how success works in college or anywhere else.

For first-gen students, this can be especially challenging. You may not have grown up seeing people networking or seek mentors. Your family might highly value self-reliance and see asking for help as a sign of weakness. The hidden curriculum of college—all those unwritten rules we've talked about—includes the expectation that you'll build relationships with professors and staff. Nobody explains this directly, but it's crucial for your success. Let me explain it now so you know.

Why Relationships Matter So Much

In my research, relationships came up again and again as a deciding factor in whether students persisted to graduation. When I asked students what helped them stay in college when things got tough, the answers were remarkably consistent. A mentor who believed in them when they doubted themselves. A study group that kept them accountable and motivated. A professor who noticed they were struggling and reached out. A friend who understood what they were going through. An advisor who helped them navigate a crisis they couldn't handle alone.

Research by Smith and Tinto in 2022 confirmed what students told me in my own research: belonging matters enormously for student success. Students who feel connected to their institution—who feel like they're part of a community, like people know them and care about them, like they matter—

are much more likely to persist than students who feel isolated and invisible. This sense of belonging affects everything: your motivation to show up, your mental health, your academic performance, and ultimately your decision to stay or leave.

> *"There were so many times I almost dropped out. What kept me going wasn't my own determination—it was the people who wouldn't let me quit. My advisor checked in on me regularly. My roommate noticed when I was down and dragged me to dinner. My study group expected me to show up. I stayed for them as much as for myself."*
>
> *—First-generation college student*

Think about what this student is saying. She didn't persist through pure willpower or individual grit. She persisted because she was embedded in a web of relationships that held her up when she couldn't hold herself up. That's not weakness—that's how humans actually work. We're social creatures. We evolved to depend on each other. We genuinely do better when we're connected to others who care about us.

For first-gen students, the belonging piece can be extra complicated. You might feel like an outsider, like you don't quite fit in with students who seem to know all the unwritten rules automatically. You might look around and wonder if you really belong here or if someone made a mistake letting you in. These feelings are common among first-gen students, but they're also dangerous. If you let them isolate you from others, they become self-fulfilling. Building relationships is how you fight back against those feelings of not belonging.

Relationships provide more than just emotional support, though that matters a lot. They also provide practical help—someone who can explain how things work, share notes from a class you missed, tell you about opportunities you wouldn't have heard about otherwise. They provide accountability—people who expect you to show up and notice when you don't. They provide motivation—reasons to keep going that extend beyond yourself. All of these matter tremendously for your success.

The Support Network You Need

Not all relationships serve the same purpose in your life. To build a strong support network, you need different kinds of connections that serve different needs at different times. Think of it like building a team where each person plays a different position. You need the whole team working together to succeed.

First, you need mentors—people who have been where you're going and can show you the way. Mentors give you advice based on their experience, open doors to opportunities, and help you see possibilities you might not see on your own. They believe in you, sometimes before you believe in yourself. For first-gen students, mentors are especially important because they can teach you the hidden curriculum that others learned at home without even realizing they were learning it.

> *"My mentor changed my life. She was the first person in her family to go to college too, so she understood exactly what I was going through. She taught me things nobody else would have thought to explain—like how to talk to professors without feeling intimidated, how to ask for recommendation letters, how to even think about graduate school as a possibility for someone like me. I wouldn't be where I am without her guidance."*
>
> *—First-generation college student*

Second, you need peers—people going through the same experience alongside you right now. Peers provide companionship, study partners, and the comfort of knowing you're not alone in your struggles. They understand what you're going through in a way that people outside college really can't. They can share tips and information about classes and professors. And they can keep you accountable—when you're part of a study group, you show up because others are counting on you to be there.

> *"My study group saved my grades and my sanity. We met every week, same time, same place. Just knowing that other people were struggling with the same material made me feel so much better about my own struggles. We pushed each other to do better. When one person wanted to give up, the others wouldn't let them."*
>
> *—First-generation college student*

Third, you need professors and staff who know you by name. These are the people who can write recommendation letters that actually say something meaningful about you, connect you to opportunities and internships, and intervene when you're struggling academically. But they can only help you if they actually know who you are. That means going to office hours, participating in class, and making yourself visible. Many first-gen students stay invisible because they don't realize how important these relationships are.

> *"I was terrified to go to office hours at first. I thought professors were too important and too busy to talk to someone like me. But once I finally pushed myself to start going, everything changed. My professor became my advisor, then my mentor. She recommended me for an internship that completely changed my career path. None of that would have happened if I'd stayed invisible."*
>
> *—First-generation college student*

Fourth, you need connections to support services—the tutoring center, writing center, counseling center, financial aid office, and other resources on your campus. These aren't just anonymous services; they're staffed by real people who genuinely want to help you succeed. Building relationships with these staff members means you have someone specific to turn to when particular problems arise, someone who already knows your situation.

Finally, you need your home relationships—family and friends from before college. These relationships anchor you to who you are and where you came from. They remind you why you're doing this in the first place. They provide support and love that campus relationships simply can't replace. But these relationships may also need to evolve as you change, which can be complicated and sometimes painful. We'll talk more about this important topic later in the chapter.

Connecting with Professors

For many first-gen students, the idea of building a relationship with a professor feels strange or even inappropriate. Professors seem so busy, so important, so far above you in the hierarchy. Why would they want to talk to you? This thinking is completely understandable given where you're coming from, but it's also wrong. Most professors genuinely want to connect with students. That's actually part of why they chose this career in the first place. But they can't connect with you if you never give them the chance.

Office hours exist specifically for students to come talk to professors. That's literally what they're for. You're not bothering anyone by showing up. You're using the system exactly as it's designed to be used. Many professors are actually disappointed when students don't come to office hours. They sit there waiting, wanting to help, but students don't come. They can't help students they never see or talk to.

Research by Schwartz and colleagues in 2021 found that mentoring relationships—including relationships with professors—significantly impact student success. Students who have meaningful connections with faculty members show better academic performance and higher persistence rates compared to students who remain anonymous. These relationships really do matter, and they're worth the initial awkwardness of building them.

> *"I made a rule for myself at the start of the semester: I had to go to every professor's office hours at least once in the first two weeks. Just to introduce myself, nothing more. It felt so awkward the first time—I didn't even know what to say. But it got easier with practice. By the end of the semester, I actually looked forward to those conversations. And when I needed recommendations later, I had professors who actually knew me as a person."*
>
> *—First-generation college student*

What do you actually talk about in office hours? You can ask questions about the course material you're confused about. You can ask for feedback on your work or how to improve. You can ask about the professor's research or career path if you're interested. You can ask for advice about your own academic or career plans. The specific topic honestly matters less than the act of showing up and making a human connection. Over time, these brief interactions build into a real relationship.

Don't wait until you're already in crisis to visit office hours. By then, you're asking for help from someone who doesn't know you at all. It's much better to build the relationship when things are going well, so you have someone to turn to when things inevitably get hard. Think of it as an investment that pays off later when you need it most.

Participating in class is another way to become visible to professors. Ask questions when you're confused. Offer your thoughts during discussions. Show that you're engaged with the material and thinking about it. Professors notice and remember students who participate, and they think of them when opportunities arise. You don't have to be the smartest person in the room—you just have to be present, engaged, and willing to contribute.

Finding Your People

Finding peers who support your success can feel genuinely challenging, especially if you're naturally introverted or if you feel like you don't quite fit in with other students. But peer relationships are too important to just leave to chance and hope for the best. You need to be intentional and proactive about building them.

One of the best ways to build peer relationships is through structured activities—study groups, student organizations, campus jobs, intramural sports, or classes with group projects. These give you a built-in reason to interact with people and something concrete to talk about together. The friendship often grows naturally from the shared activity over time.

> *"I joined a student organization related to my major, and that's where I found my people. We had something in common right away—we were all interested in the same field and thinking about similar careers. The friendships grew from there organically. Now some of them are my closest friends, and we push each other to succeed every day."*
>
> *—First-generation college student*

Study groups are particularly valuable because they combine academic support with social connection at the same time. You're helping each other learn while also building relationships. When you study with others, you're accountable to them—you prepare because you don't want to let the group down or look unprepared. And you benefit from their knowledge and perspectives, not just your own limited view of the material.

If there isn't already a study group for your class, start one yourself. It's easier than you might think. Just ask a few people after class if they want to study together sometime. Most students are looking for connection just like you are. They're just waiting for someone else to make the first move because it feels scary. Be that person who makes the first move.

> *"I was so lonely my first semester. I thought everyone else had friends already and I was the only one struggling to connect with people. Then I decided to just start inviting people to study with me, even though it felt awkward. Turns out lots of people felt exactly the same way I did—they were just waiting for someone else to reach out first. I realized I wasn't the only lonely one."*
>
> *—First-generation college student*

Be strategic about the peers you spend significant time with. Relationships powerfully shape behavior in ways you might not even notice. If you hang out with people who skip class regularly and don't take school seriously, you'll be pulled in that direction over time. If you hang out with people who are committed to succeeding, their positive habits will rub off on you. This doesn't mean dropping all your current friends—it just means being aware of how people influence you and making sure you have people in your life who actively support your goals.

Research by Museus and Chang in 2021 emphasized that peer connections play a crucial role in student persistence. The sense of belonging that comes from peer relationships—feeling like you're part of a community, like people know you and value you—is a powerful force keeping students enrolled and engaged even when things get difficult.

Staying Connected to Home

While you're building new relationships at college, you also need to maintain your important relationships back home. This balancing act can get complicated. You're changing and growing, and the people at home may not fully understand or appreciate those changes. You might feel pulled between two worlds that don't quite understand each other.

Research by Roksa and Kinsley in 2019 found that family support—particularly emotional support—significantly impacts whether students persist to graduation. What matters most isn't whether your family can help with homework or explain how college works. What matters is whether they believe in you and support your journey, even when they don't fully understand what you're going through or why you're making certain choices.

> *"My parents don't really get what I'm doing in college. They can't help with my classes or my career planning because they've never experienced any of it. But they believe in me completely and totally. When I call home stressed out and ready to quit, my mom just says, 'You got this, mija. We're so proud of you.' That belief keeps me going more than any specific advice ever could."*
>
> *—First-generation college student*

Stay in regular contact with the people who matter to you at home. This might be phone calls, texts, video chats, or visits when you can manage them. The specific method matters less than the consistency of staying in touch. Let them know what's happening in your life—both the struggles and the victories. Help them understand your world, even if they can't fully enter it themselves.

At the same time, be prepared for some tension. As you

change and grow during college, your relationships back home will naturally change too. Old friends might feel like you're leaving them behind or becoming a different person. Family members might not understand your new priorities or the person you're becoming. You might find yourself speaking differently or thinking differently, and that can create distance and discomfort.

> *"Going home for breaks got harder as college went on. I'd changed so much, and my old friends really hadn't. We didn't have as much in common anymore, and conversations felt forced. It made me sad, but I also realized that growing apart from some people was part of growing into who I was supposed to become."*
>
> *—First-generation college student*

This tension is normal and almost universal among students who are growing and changing, but it can still be painful. The key is not to cut off one world entirely for the other. You don't have to choose between your college life and your home life as if they're mutually exclusive. You can bridge both worlds, even if it takes real effort and intentionality. Bring your worlds together when you can—tell your college friends about home, tell your home friends about college. Be patient with people who don't understand your journey. Remember that their confusion and sometimes their resistance often comes from love.

Some first-gen students feel guilty about the opportunities they have that others don't. Your family sacrificed so you could be here. Your friends back home might not have had the same chances you did. That guilt is natural and understandable, but don't let it sabotage your success. The best way to honor their sacrifices is to succeed, not to hold yourself back out of misplaced guilt. And your success might actually open doors for others who come after you.

The Art of Asking for Help

Asking for help can be genuinely hard, especially if you've been taught to be self-reliant or if you're worried about looking weak or incompetent in front of others. But learning to ask for help effectively is one of the most important skills you can develop in college and beyond. The students who succeed aren't the ones who figure everything out completely alone. They're the ones who know how to get help when they need it.

Research by Delmas and Childs in 2021 showed that early alert systems—where faculty and staff proactively reach out to students who appear to be struggling—help connect students with support before small problems become full-blown crises. But these systems only work if students actually respond to the outreach and accept the help being offered. Too many students ignore offers of help because they're embarrassed or think they should be able to handle things completely on their own.

> *"I grew up believing that asking for help meant you were weak. Real strength meant handling everything yourself without complaining. College taught me that belief is completely backwards. The smartest, most successful people I met were constantly asking for help—from professors, from tutors, from advisors, from each other. They weren't weak at all; they were strategic about using every available resource."*
>
> *—First-generation college student*

Reframe how you think about help. Asking for help isn't admitting failure or incompetence. It's using available resources wisely and strategically. It's being smart about your success. Think of it this way: if you were trying to build a house, would you insist on doing it completely without any tools? Of course not—that would be foolish. Support services, mentors, and advisors are tools for building your success. Using them isn't weakness—it's wisdom and strategic thinking.

Be specific when you ask for help. 'I'm struggling' is a start, but 'I don't understand how to set up the equation for problem 5 on the homework' gives someone something concrete and specific to help with. The more specific you are about what exactly you need, the more effective the help will be. Think carefully about what you're actually stuck on before you ask.

Follow through when help is offered to you. If an advisor suggests you visit the tutoring center, actually go there. If a professor offers extra office hours, show up for them. If a friend offers to study with you, follow through on the plan. People eventually stop offering help to those who don't actually take it. Show that you're serious about getting support, and more support will naturally come your way.

> *"The tutoring center changed everything for me academically. I put off going for so long because I thought it was only for people who were really failing badly. Turns out, lots of successful students use it regularly to stay ahead. It's not about being desperate—it's about getting better continuously. I wish I'd gone so much sooner."*
>
> *—First-generation college student*

Finding and Working with Mentors

A mentor is someone who has been where you want to go and can help you get there. They offer guidance based on experience, open doors to opportunities, share wisdom from what they've learned, and sometimes just believe in you when you're having trouble believing in yourself. For first-gen students, mentors are especially valuable because they can teach you things that others learned at home without even knowing they were learning them.

Mentors can be professors, advisors, supervisors at work or internships, professionals working in your field, or even older students who have already navigated what you're going through now. The key is finding someone who has knowledge and experience you can genuinely learn from and who is willing to invest their time and energy in your development.

Research by Palmer and Maramba in 2021 highlighted the importance of mentorship for student success, particularly for students from underrepresented backgrounds. Having someone who believes in you and actively supports your development makes a measurable, significant difference in outcomes.

> *"My mentor saw things in me I couldn't see in myself. When I doubted whether I could handle graduate school, she reminded me of everything I'd already accomplished against the odds. When I didn't know how to navigate tricky professional situations, she coached me through them step by step. She opened doors I didn't even know existed."*
>
> *—First-generation college student*

How do you actually find a mentor? Start by being a good mentee—someone worth investing in. Show up consistently and reliably. Be prepared when you meet. Follow through on advice you're given. Express genuine gratitude for their time. Make it easy and rewarding for someone to invest in you. People want to mentor students who are committed and appreciative, who will actually use the help they're being given.

Don't be afraid to directly ask someone to be your mentor. Many people are genuinely honored to be asked and really do want to help the next generation succeed. You might say something like, 'I really admire your career path. Would you be willing to meet with me occasionally to give me advice?' Most people will say yes, and the worst that happens if they say no is that you're in exactly the same place you started.

A mentoring relationship develops over time through regular contact. It's not a one-time conversation—it's an ongoing relationship where you check in periodically, ask questions, share updates on your progress, and build trust together. The relationship gets richer and more valuable as it develops over months and years. Your mentor gets to know you better and can give increasingly personalized advice.

Creating Your Sense of Belonging

Belonging isn't just about having individual relationships. It's about feeling like you're part of something larger than yourself—that you fit here, that you matter, that this place is genuinely for people like you. For first-gen students, building this sense of belonging can take extra effort because you might start out feeling like an outsider looking in.

Research consistently shows that sense of belonging is one of the strongest predictors of student success. Students who feel they truly belong persist at higher rates, earn better grades, and report better mental health than those who feel like outsiders. Creating belonging isn't a luxury or a nice-to-have—it's essential for your success and wellbeing.

Belonging is built through repeated positive interactions over time. Every time you have a good conversation with a professor, you belong a little more. Every time your study group accomplishes something together, you belong a little more. Every time someone on campus knows your name and smiles when they see you, you belong a little more. These small moments accumulate into something powerful.

> *"I didn't feel like I belonged for most of my first year. I felt like everyone else knew what they were doing and I was just faking it and hoping not to get caught. The turning point was joining a first-gen student group. Suddenly I was with people*

> *who understood exactly what my experience was like. We built each other up. For the first time, I felt like I was actually supposed to be here."*
>
> *—First-generation college student*

Seek out spaces where you feel welcome and accepted. This might be a student organization, a cultural center, a regular study spot where you see familiar faces, or just a group of people who accept you as you are. These spaces of belonging give you a home base on campus where you don't have to prove yourself or explain your background.

Remember that belonging is something you actively create, not just something you passively find or wait for. You build belonging by showing up, contributing, and investing in community. The more you participate, the more you belong. The more you belong, the more you want to participate. It's an upward spiral that feeds on itself.

What Research Helps Us Understand

Research consistently identifies relationships as a crucial factor in student persistence and success. Students who feel a sense of belonging—connection to peers, mentors, faculty, and the institution itself—show higher persistence rates, better academic outcomes, and stronger wellbeing. For first-gen students, mentoring relationships are particularly impactful, helping students navigate the hidden curriculum and see possibilities they might not otherwise recognize. Family support, especially emotional support and belief in the student, predicts persistence even when families cannot provide practical academic help. Building and maintaining a network of supportive relationships is not a distraction from academic work—it is a foundation that makes academic success possible.

The Huddle

Take time to reflect on these questions thoughtfully, alone or with others.

Take time alone or with others to work through these questions. They build on each other to help you map and strengthen your support network.

Begin by considering this: list the five types of relationships discussed in this chapter that form a support network. Which ones do you currently have? Which are missing?

Next, reflect on this: explain in your own words why asking for help is a strength rather than a weakness. How does reframing help-seeking change how you approach it?

Take a moment to think about this: choose one professor you have this semester. Make a specific plan to visit their office hours this week—what will you talk about? What's one question you could ask?

Consider this honestly: think about your current peer relationships. Which ones actively support your success? Which ones might be pulling you away from your goals? What patterns do you notice?

Now ask yourself: assess your relationship with your family and home community since starting college. What's working well? What tensions have you noticed? How are you bridging your two worlds?

Reflect carefully on this: design your ideal support network. Who would be in it? What role would each person play? What's one concrete step you can take this week to build toward that network?

Finally, consider this: write a brief message to someone who has supported you in college—a mentor, professor, friend, or family member. Tell them specifically what their support has meant to you.

Relationships sustain you through challenges, but challenges will still come. Chapter 5 explores how to build resilience—the capacity to persist through difficulty and come back stronger.

CHAPTER 5

Building Resilience: Persisting Through Difficulty

"I failed my first college exam. I remember sitting in the hallway afterward, convinced I had made a terrible mistake coming here. But I didn't quit. I figured out what went wrong, got help, and passed the class. That failure taught me more about myself than any success ever did."

—First-generation college student

As discussed in Chapter 1, resilience is not just academic survival. It is professional signal formation. You will face hard times in college. That's not pessimism—it's reality. Everyone who makes it through encounters moments when they want to give up. Failed exams. Overwhelming stress. Family crises that pull your attention away from school. Financial struggles that make you wonder if you can afford to stay. Moments of doubt so deep they shake your sense of who you are and whether you belong here. The question isn't whether hard times will come. The question is what you'll do when they arrive.

The student who opens this chapter experienced what felt like disaster—failing an exam in her first semester. In that moment, sitting in the hallway with her head in her hands, she had a choice. She could interpret the failure as proof that she didn't belong here, pack her bags, and go home. Or she could interpret it as information about what she needed to learn and change. She chose the second path. That choice made all the difference in her college career and her life.

This chapter is about resilience—the ability to persist through difficulty and come back stronger on the other side. Resilience isn't about never struggling or never feeling pain. It's about how you respond when struggles and pain inevitably arrive. It's about getting back up after you fall down, learning from setbacks instead of being destroyed by them, and finding the strength to keep going even when everything in you wants to quit.

Here's what I want you to understand from the very start: resilience is not a fixed trait you either have or don't have. It's a set of skills and mindsets that can be learned and strengthened over time with practice and intention. Some people may have had more practice building resilience before college, but everyone can develop it further. The challenges you face in college are opportunities to build resilience that will serve you for the rest of your life, long after graduation.

For first-gen students, resilience is especially important. You're navigating territory your family hasn't traveled before you. You may face challenges that students with college-educated parents don't encounter or don't encounter as intensely. You need resilience not because something is wrong with you, but because your path is genuinely harder in some real ways. The good news is that many first-gen students have already developed significant resilience through the challenges they faced before college even began. You may be stronger than you realize.

What Resilience Really Means

Resilience is often misunderstood. People think it means being tough, never showing weakness, pushing through pain without complaint. That's not resilience—that's just stubbornness, and it often leads to burnout and breakdown. True resilience is more nuanced and more sustainable than simply gritting your teeth and refusing to acknowledge difficulty.

Resilience means bouncing back from setbacks, but it also means bouncing forward—using difficulties as opportunities to grow and learn rather than just survive. It means adapting to challenges rather than just enduring them passively. It means knowing when to push through and when to step back and recover. It means asking for help when you need it, not trying to handle everything alone through sheer force of will.

Research by Rehr and colleagues in 2021 found that students who developed effective coping strategies showed stronger persistence through challenges than those who tried to muscle through without strategies. These weren't students who never struggled—they were students who had learned how to struggle productively. They had tools for managing difficulty instead of being overwhelmed by it.

> *"I used to think being strong meant never letting anyone see me struggle. I'd hide in my room when things got hard and refuse to ask for help no matter what. That wasn't strength—it was pride, and it almost cost me my education. Real strength turned out to be admitting I was struggling and letting people help me through it."*
>
> *—First-generation college student*

Resilient people aren't immune to negative emotions. They feel fear, frustration, sadness, and doubt just like everyone else does. The difference is that they don't let those emotions make their decisions for them. They feel the fear and take action anyway. They experience the doubt and keep showing up. They allow themselves to be sad but don't let sadness become a permanent state that stops them from moving forward.

Think of resilience like a muscle. Every time you face a challenge and work through it, that muscle gets a little stronger. The challenges don't necessarily get easier, but your capacity to handle them grows larger. The student who persists through a difficult first year develops resilience that helps them handle the challenges of later years with more confidence. Each difficulty overcome becomes a resource for facing the next one.

The Mindset That Makes the Difference

How you think about challenges shapes how you respond

to them. Psychologist Carol Dweck's research on mindset shows that people generally fall into two categories: those with a fixed mindset and those with a growth mindset. This distinction has profound implications for resilience and for how you'll navigate the inevitable difficulties of college.

People with a fixed mindset believe that abilities are basically set at birth—you're either smart or you're not, talented or you're not, cut out for college or not. When they encounter failure, they interpret it as evidence about who they fundamentally are. A failed exam means 'I'm not smart enough for this.' A rejected application means 'I'm not good enough.' Because they see abilities as fixed and unchangeable, failure feels permanent and threatening to their very identity.

People with a growth mindset believe that abilities can be developed through effort, strategy, and help from others. When they encounter failure, they interpret it as information about what they need to work on, not a verdict on who they are. A failed exam means 'I need to study differently or get help with this material.' A rejection means 'I need to strengthen my application for next time.' Because they see abilities as developable, failure feels temporary and useful rather than permanent and devastating.

> *"My whole life, people told me I was smart. I thought that was a good thing until college, when I started struggling for the first time. If I was smart, why was I failing? It messed with my head badly. Then I learned about growth mindset and realized that struggling didn't mean I wasn't smart—it meant I was learning something new and genuinely hard. That shift in thinking changed everything for me."*
>
> *—First-generation college student*

The growth mindset is essential for resilience because it

changes what failure means. With a fixed mindset, failure is a verdict: you don't have what it takes, and you never will. With a growth mindset, failure is feedback: here's what you need to work on to improve. The same event—a failed exam, a rejected application, a difficult semester—leads to completely different responses depending on which mindset you bring to it.

Research by Yeager and colleagues in 2022 showed that mindset interventions—teaching students about the growth mindset and how the brain can change—improved academic outcomes, particularly for students from disadvantaged backgrounds. Simply learning that the brain can grow and change, that struggle is a normal part of learning rather than a sign of inadequacy, made a real measurable difference in how students performed and whether they persisted.

The good news is that mindset can be changed even if you've had a fixed mindset your whole life. Even if you've spent years believing that abilities are set in stone, you can learn to adopt a growth mindset. It starts with paying attention to your self-talk —the things you say to yourself inside your own head. When you hear yourself thinking 'I'm just not good at this,' try adding the word 'yet': 'I'm not good at this yet.' That small addition opens up the possibility of growth and change.

The Challenges You'll Face

Let's be honest about what you're up against. College brings specific challenges, and first-gen students often face additional ones that their peers don't encounter. Knowing what to expect doesn't make challenges disappear, but it does help you prepare and respond more effectively when they inevitably arrive.

Academic challenges are often the most visible and immediate. The work is harder than high school. The pace is faster. The expectations are higher. You may encounter subjects that don't come easily to you, professors whose teaching style doesn't match your learning style, or exams that seem designed to trip you up. Almost everyone struggles academically at some point in their college career.

> *"I breezed through high school without really trying hard. College was a complete shock to my system. Suddenly I was working harder than I ever had in my life and still barely passing some classes. I had to completely rebuild how I approached learning from the ground up. It was humbling, but it was also where I really grew as a person."*
>
> *—First-generation college student*

Financial challenges affect many students but hit first-gen students especially hard. You may be working significant hours at a job while trying to study and keep up with classes. You may worry about money constantly, with that stress always in the background of everything else. You may face unexpected expenses that derail your plans—a car repair, a medical bill, a family emergency. Financial stress doesn't just affect your bank account—it affects your mental health, your sleep quality, your ability to focus on schoolwork, and your overall capacity to succeed.

Family challenges can be particularly complicated for first-gen students. Your family may not understand the demands of college—how much time studying takes, why you can't come home every weekend, what you're actually doing all day. They may expect you to be available for responsibilities at home that conflict with your studies. They may be dealing with their own crises that pull you away from school. You might feel torn between your obligations at home and your goals at college, with no clear right answer.

> *"My mom got really sick during my sophomore year. I wanted to drop out immediately and go home to help take care of her. My advisor helped me find a way to reduce my course load and still*

> *stay enrolled instead. It was the hardest semester of my entire life, but I made it through. I learned I was capable of handling way more than I ever thought possible."*
>
> *—First-generation college student*

Mental health challenges are extremely common in college. The stress, the transitions, the pressure to succeed, the distance from home—they all take a real toll. Anxiety, depression, loneliness, and burnout affect many students at some point during their college years. These aren't signs of weakness or character flaws. They're signs that you're human and facing real challenges. What matters is recognizing when you're struggling and getting the help you need.

Identity challenges can be particularly intense for first-gen students. You're caught between two worlds—the world you came from and the world you're entering. You may feel like you don't fully belong in either place. You may feel guilty about the opportunities your family and friends back home don't have. You may struggle to integrate who you were with who you're becoming. This kind of identity work is hard and ongoing.

Research by McNaughton-Cassill and colleagues in 2021 documented the strong connection between stress and academic performance. Students who learned to actively manage their stress showed better outcomes than those who tried to just push through without addressing it. Managing challenges isn't optional or a luxury—it's essential for success.

Strategies for Building Resilience

Resilience isn't just about having the right mindset, though mindset matters a lot. It's also about having concrete strategies and practices for dealing with difficulty when it arrives. Here are specific approaches that research and experience have shown to build resilience in college students.

First, reframe how you think about challenges. Instead of

asking 'Why is this happening to me?' ask 'What can I learn from this?' Instead of seeing obstacles as stop signs that block your path, see them as puzzles to solve or detours to navigate. This reframing doesn't deny that challenges are hard or pretend that pain doesn't hurt. It just changes your relationship to difficulty —from victim to problem-solver, from passive to active.

Second, break big problems into smaller pieces. When you're overwhelmed, everything feels impossible and insurmountable. But almost any challenge becomes more manageable when you break it down into smaller steps. Failing a class feels catastrophic and final. But what's the next small step you can actually take? Maybe it's emailing the professor to ask about extra credit opportunities. Maybe it's finding a tutor for the material you're struggling with. Focus on the next small step, not the whole mountain you need to climb.

> *"When I was at my lowest point and ready to quit everything, my counselor taught me to just focus on getting through the next hour. Not the next week, not even the next day—just the next hour. That made it manageable when nothing else did. One hour at a time, I got through the crisis. Eventually the hours added up to days, and the days added up to getting better."*
>
> *—First-generation college student*

Third, build and actively use your support network. We talked in the last chapter about building relationships. When challenges hit, those relationships become lifelines that can save you. Don't isolate yourself when things get hard—that's actually when you need people most. Reach out to friends, mentors, family, counselors. Let people help you. You don't have to face difficulties alone, and trying to do so often makes everything worse.

Fourth, take care of your physical foundation. When you're stressed, it's tempting to skip sleep, eat junk food, stop exercising, and let basic self-care slide. But these behaviors make everything worse, not better. Your body and mind are deeply connected. Getting enough sleep, eating reasonably well, and moving your body all build your capacity to handle stress. They're not luxuries or extras—they're necessities for resilience that you can't afford to skip.

Fifth, maintain perspective. In the middle of a crisis, everything feels urgent and permanent, like it will last forever. But most of what feels catastrophic in the moment looks very different with time and distance. Will this matter in five years? Will you even remember it? Often the answer is no. Keeping perspective doesn't minimize real pain or pretend problems aren't serious, but it helps you avoid making permanent decisions based on temporary feelings.

> *"My advisor told me something I've never forgotten: 'This semester is not your whole life.' When I was failing and ready to quit everything, that reminder helped me see the bigger picture. One bad semester didn't have to define my entire future or determine who I'd become. I could recover from this setback."*
>
> *—First-generation college student*

Sixth, practice self-compassion. When you're struggling, your inner critic often gets loud and harsh. You beat yourself up for not being better, stronger, smarter—for not handling things the way you think you should. But research shows that self-compassion—treating yourself with the same kindness you'd show a good friend—actually builds resilience better than self-criticism does. Talk to yourself the way you'd talk to someone you love who was going through a hard time.

Knowing When to Seek Help

There's an important difference between challenges you can handle on your own with basic coping strategies and challenges that require professional support to navigate. Part of resilience is knowing which situation you're in and being willing to seek help when you genuinely need it.

Normal stress looks like: feeling overwhelmed during finals week, being nervous before a big presentation, having a hard day after getting a bad grade. These feelings are unpleasant but temporary. They respond to basic coping strategies—rest, support from friends, taking a break, using the techniques in this chapter.

Warning signs that you need more professional support include: persistent sadness that doesn't lift after a few weeks, anxiety that interferes with your ability to function day to day, significant changes in sleep or appetite that last more than a couple weeks, thoughts of harming yourself, feeling hopeless about the future, using substances to cope with difficult feelings, withdrawing completely from everyone and everything. These are signs to reach out for professional help, not signs to try harder on your own.

Most college campuses have counseling services specifically designed to help students through difficult times. These services are usually free or very low-cost for enrolled students. Using them isn't a sign of weakness or failure—it's a sign of wisdom and self-awareness. The strongest students know when they need help and aren't too proud or ashamed to ask for it.

> *"Going to counseling was honestly the best decision I made in all four years of college. I waited way too long because I thought I should be able to handle things myself, like something was wrong with me for needing help. When I finally went, I realized I'd been carrying so much weight that I didn't have to carry alone. Counseling gave me tools and perspectives I still use years after graduating."*
>
> *—First-generation college student*

Research by Delmas and Childs in 2021 showed that early intervention—getting help before small problems become big crises—significantly improves outcomes compared to waiting until crisis point. Don't wait until you're in complete crisis mode to reach out. If you're struggling, talk to someone now. It's much easier to address challenges early than to climb out of a deep hole later.

Besides counseling, there are other campus resources for specific types of challenges. Financial aid offices can help with money problems. Academic advisors can help you navigate academic difficulties and make plans. Disability services can provide accommodations if you have a documented condition. Health services can address physical health concerns. Know what resources exist on your campus and use them when you need them.

The Gift of Failure

Nobody wants to fail. Failure hurts. It's embarrassing and discouraging. But here's something that might surprise you: failure is often one of the most valuable experiences you can have. The students I've worked with who achieved the most long-term success weren't the ones who never failed. They were the ones who failed, learned from it, and came back stronger on the other side.

Failure teaches you things that success simply can't. When everything goes smoothly, you don't have to examine your strategies or strengthen your weaknesses. You just coast along on what's already working. But when you fail, you're forced to look honestly at what went wrong. You identify gaps in your knowledge or your approach. You develop new strategies that wouldn't have occurred to you otherwise. You grow in ways that easy success would never require.

> *"My biggest failure in college—nearly flunking out my entire first year—became my biggest teacher. It forced me to completely change how*

> *I approached school at every level. I developed study habits, time management skills, and self-awareness that I never would have built if things had come easily to me. I'm actually grateful for that failure now, as strange as that sounds."*
>
> *—First-generation college student*

Failure also builds resilience directly through experience. Each time you fail and then recover, you prove to yourself that failure isn't fatal. You learn from lived experience that you can survive disappointment, adapt to setbacks, and continue moving forward. This knowledge becomes a resource you carry with you into every future challenge. The next time you face potential failure, you know from your own experience that you can handle it.

The key is how you process failure—whether you do it productively or unproductively. Productive failure involves honest reflection: What happened? What was in my control and what wasn't? What would I do differently? What did I learn that I can use going forward? It involves taking appropriate responsibility without excessive self-blame. It involves making concrete changes based on what you learned. It involves moving forward rather than getting stuck in regret about the past.

Unproductive failure involves denial, blame, or shame. Denial means refusing to acknowledge that anything really went wrong—making excuses or minimizing what happened. Blame means putting all responsibility on external factors—the unfair professor, the impossible test, the circumstances beyond your control. Shame means making the failure about your fundamental identity—'I'm a failure as a person'—rather than about a specific event that happened. These responses prevent learning and growth and keep you stuck.

Try to see failure as data rather than as judgment. A failed exam doesn't mean you're stupid or don't belong in college. It means your preparation wasn't effective for this particular test in this particular subject. That's actually useful information you can work with. Now you can figure out what kind of preparation would work better next time. Failure becomes feedback that helps you improve rather than a verdict that defines you.

Building Your Resilience Over Time

Resilience isn't built in a single day or through a single experience. It develops over time through repeated experiences of facing challenges, working through them, and coming out the other side. You can accelerate this development by being intentional about how you approach difficulties rather than just letting them happen to you.

Start by taking on appropriate challenges—ones that stretch you but don't overwhelm you completely. Growth happens at the edge of your comfort zone—not in the safe and easy center, but also not in the overwhelming outer territory where you can't function. Seek out challenges that push you while remaining manageable. Each challenge you meet successfully builds confidence and capacity for the next, bigger one.

Reflect regularly on what you've already overcome in your life. It's easy to forget how much you've already handled and survived. When you're facing a new challenge, remind yourself of past challenges you've navigated successfully. You survived those difficult times. You'll survive this one too. Your history of resilience is real evidence for your future resilience.

> *"I started keeping a list of hard things I'd gotten through—a resilience journal, basically. Every time I felt like I couldn't handle something new, I looked at that list. If I could survive my parents' divorce, multiple financial aid disasters, and nearly failing calculus, I could probably handle whatever new thing was scaring me. That list gave me courage."*
>
> *—First-generation college student*

Develop your own resilience rituals—practices that help you recover when you're knocked down. This might be calling a specific person who always helps you feel better, going for a run or a long walk, journaling about what you're experiencing, listening to particular music, or watching a favorite movie that comforts you. Know what helps you bounce back, and make sure you actually do those things when you need them instead of just suffering.

Research by Bennett and colleagues in 2022 emphasized that student success depends on both individual capacity and institutional support working together. You can build your personal resilience through the strategies in this chapter, but also take full advantage of the support structures your college offers. You don't have to do this alone, and trying to do it completely alone often backfires.

Finally, remember that developing resilience is itself a form of success, separate from any external outcomes. Every time you face a challenge and keep going, you're succeeding—even if the external outcome isn't what you hoped for. The grade matters, but so does the growth. Sometimes the most important thing you'll get from a difficult experience isn't the external result at all. It's the internal development that no one can see but you.

Writing Your Resilience Story

Everyone who makes it through college has a resilience story—moments when they faced real difficulty and found a way through it. Your story is still being written. The challenges you face now are the chapters that will inspire and sustain you later in life.

Think about the first-gen students who came before you and graduated. They faced many of the same challenges you're facing right now. They felt the same doubts, encountered the same obstacles, experienced the same moments of wanting to give up on everything. But they persisted anyway. They found their way through. They graduated and built lives they're proud of. You can join them in that story.

Your background as a first-gen student isn't just a source of challenges. It's also a source of genuine strength. You've likely already overcome significant obstacles just to get here in the first place. You have grit and determination that was forged long before college even began. The resilience you're building now adds to resilience you already have from your life before this.

> *"When I finally graduated, I looked back at everything I'd been through to get there—the failures, the financial stress, the family crises, all the moments I almost quit. All of it was part of my story. I didn't just earn a degree. I proved to myself that I could handle genuinely hard things. That knowledge was worth as much to me as the diploma itself."*
>
> *—First-generation college student*

The difficulties you face in college are real, but they're not permanent. They're chapters in your story, not the whole book. And the ending of your story—the person you become, the life you build—is still unwritten. You get to write it through the choices you make every day. The struggles of today become the strength of tomorrow. Keep going. Keep growing. Your resilience story is still being written, and it can be a story of triumph over real adversity.

What Research Helps Us Understand

Research on resilience shows that it is not a fixed trait but a set of skills and mindsets that can be developed over time with practice and intention. Students who adopt a growth mindset—believing that abilities can be developed through effort—show greater persistence through challenges. Effective coping strategies, social support, and self-compassion all contribute to resilient outcomes. Early intervention when problems arise leads to better results than waiting until crisis point. Failure, when processed productively, can be a powerful teacher that builds both skill and resilience. First-gen students who develop strong resilience show persistence rates comparable to their continuing-generation peers.

The Huddle

Take time to reflect on these questions thoughtfully, alone or with others.

Take time alone or with others to work through these questions. They build on each other to help you develop your resilience capacity.

Begin by considering this: what is the difference between a fixed mindset and a growth mindset? How does each mindset interpret failure differently?

Next, reflect on this: explain in your own words why failure can be valuable. What does failure teach that success cannot?

Take a moment to think about this: think about a recent challenge or setback you faced. How did you respond? Using strategies from this chapter, what might you do differently next time?

Consider this honestly: examine your self-talk when things go wrong. Do you tend toward self-criticism or self-compassion? Fixed mindset or growth mindset? What patterns do you notice?

Now ask yourself: assess your current coping strategies. Which ones serve you well? Which ones might actually make things worse? What's one strategy you could add to your toolkit?

Reflect carefully on this: write your resilience story so far—the challenges you've overcome to get here. How might this history be a resource for facing future challenges?

Finally, consider this: create a personal resilience plan. What will you do when you face your next significant challenge? Who will you reach out to? What strategies will you use? How will you maintain perspective?

Resilience carries you through challenges, but success also requires knowing where you're headed. Chapter 6 brings everything together and helps you chart your path forward with purpose and intention.

CHAPTER 6

Planning Your Way Forward

Charting Your Path Forward

> *"Looking back, I can see how everything connected—the struggles, the growth, the relationships, the moments I almost quit. It all led somewhere. Now I'm not just surviving college. I'm building a life I actually want. And I finally believe I deserve it."*
>
> *—First-generation college student*

You've come a long way through this book. We've explored how college changes you and why that change matters for who you're becoming. We've looked at how to understand your unique way of learning and build study strategies that actually work according to what research tells us. We've talked about habits that sustain success when motivation inevitably fades, relationships that hold you up when you want to fall, and resilience that carries you through the hard times that will definitely come. Now it's time to bring it all together and look forward at the path ahead.

This final chapter is about charting your path forward with intention and purpose. It's about taking everything you've learned—not just from this book, but from your own lived experience—and using it to build a life you're genuinely proud of. It's about seeing the bigger picture of why you're here and where you're going, even when daily pressures make it hard to see beyond the next assignment or the next exam staring you down.

The student who opens this chapter has reached a turning point that many students eventually reach. She's no longer just surviving day to day, just getting through each week. She's building something on purpose, with intention. She can see how all the pieces of her experience connect into a larger story that makes sense. And crucially, she believes she deserves the life she's creating. That belief matters more than you might think.

For first-gen students, this forward-looking perspective can be both exciting and genuinely scary. You're charting territory your family hasn't mapped before you. The possibilities ahead of you might be broader than anything you imagined growing up in your community. But that openness can also feel overwhelming and paralyzing. When you could go anywhere, how do you choose where to go? When no one in your family has walked this particular path, how do you know if you're heading in the right direction?

This chapter won't give you all the answers—no book can do that, and anyone who promises otherwise isn't being honest. But it will give you frameworks for thinking about your future, tools for making decisions when the path isn't clear, and encouragement to dream bigger than you might have allowed yourself to dream before now. Your path forward is yours to create. Let's talk about how to create it well and with intention.

Bringing It All Together

Before we look forward at what's ahead, let's look back at what we've covered and how it all connects into a coherent whole. Each chapter built on the ones before it, and together they form a complete picture of what it takes to not just survive college but to genuinely thrive and grow through the entire experience.

We started with identity and purpose—understanding that college isn't just about getting a degree or checking a box. It's about becoming someone new while staying connected to who you've always been at your core. The seven vectors of development give you a map for the growth that's happening inside you, whether you notice it in the moment or not. First-gen students navigate this growth while also bridging two worlds that don't always understand each other, which makes the journey both harder and ultimately richer.

Then we explored your unique wiring—how your brain actually learns, what study strategies work according to research instead of just tradition, and how to build an approach that fits your particular mind instead of fighting against it. We named the hidden curriculum that no one explains but everyone is expected to know, and we talked about how understanding these unwritten rules gives you real power to navigate them successfully.

Next came habits—the systems that carry you forward when motivation disappears, as it always eventually does. We learned about the habit loop and how your brain automates behavior, the power of starting small instead of trying to change everything at once, and how environment shapes behavior more powerfully than willpower ever can. Building good habits isn't about being naturally disciplined; it's about being strategic and designing your life to make success the default path.

Then we talked about relationships—the connections that sustain you through difficulty and make success meaningful when you achieve it. Mentors, peers, professors, support services, and your people back home all play different but essential roles in your support network. Asking for help isn't weakness or something to be ashamed of; it's wisdom. No one succeeds alone, and trying to do so usually backfires.

Finally, we explored resilience—the capacity to persist through difficulty and come back stronger on the other side. We learned about growth mindset and how your beliefs about ability shape your response to challenge, strategies for managing difficulties when they arrive, when to seek professional help, and how failure can be one of your greatest teachers if you process it productively instead of destructively.

"I used to see all these things as completely separate

—studying, relationships, mental health, my sense of purpose. Now I understand they're all deeply connected to each other. When one area suffers, the others feel it too. When one area gets stronger, it lifts everything else up. It's all one system, and I'm learning to take care of the whole thing together."

—First-generation college student

These elements work together as an integrated system. Your sense of purpose motivates your habits. Your habits create time and energy for relationships. Your relationships provide support for building resilience. Your resilience helps you persist through challenges to your identity. It's all connected in a web, and strengthening any part of it strengthens the whole system.

Who You're Becoming

There is something happening beneath all of this growth that is easy to miss. College is not only shaping who you are as a person. It is also shaping who you are becoming professionally.

The seven areas we just explored—competence, emotional management, interdependence, relationships, identity, purpose, and integrity—are often described as personal development. But they are also the foundation of professional formation. Long before you apply for your first job, you are building the capacities that will define how you show up in the workplace and in the world.

When you learn to manage your time, you are developing reliability. When you regulate your emotions during stress, you are strengthening your ability to lead and to work under pressure. When you navigate disagreement in a group project instead of withdrawing, you are practicing collaboration. When you clarify your values and act on them, you are shaping a professional reputation that begins forming years before anyone reads your résumé.

Many students assume professional identity starts after graduation. In reality, it begins the moment you step into college. The habits you form, the standards you hold yourself to, the way you respond to setbacks, and the relationships you cultivate all accumulate. Over time, they become part of your professional character.

Employers rarely ask about a single exam score. What they care about is whether you can think clearly, solve problems, communicate effectively, work well with others, and persist when challenges arise. Those abilities are not developed in a single class. They are built gradually through the very growth experiences you are navigating right now.

Researchers sometimes refer to this accumulation as career capital—the skills, behaviors, credibility, and self-understanding that expand your opportunities over time. Every habit you build, every resilience moment you push through, every relationship you invest in adds to that capital.

The identity work you are doing in college is not abstract. It is not separate from your future. You are not just earning a degree. You are constructing a professional self. And that construction happens daily, often in small choices that feel ordinary at the time.

Clarifying Your Purpose

We touched on purpose in the first chapter, but it deserves deeper attention as you chart your path forward into the future. Purpose is your answer to the fundamental question 'Why am I doing this?' It's what gets you out of bed on hard mornings when you'd rather stay under the covers. It's what keeps you going when every part of you wants to quit. Research consistently shows that students with a clear sense of purpose persist at higher rates and report greater satisfaction with their education and their lives overall.

Research by Klussman and colleagues in 2021 found that students who felt genuinely connected to their goals—not just going through the motions but truly believing in what they were working toward—showed stronger motivation, better attitudes toward school, and higher achievement. Purpose isn't just nice to have as an extra. It's fuel that powers everything else you do. Without it, you're running on empty and wondering why everything feels so hard.

Your purpose doesn't have to be grand or world-changing to be real and powerful for you personally. It might be: wanting to give your family a better life than they had, wanting to prove something to yourself about what you're capable of, wanting to help people in your community who are struggling, wanting to explore ideas that genuinely fascinate you, wanting to build a career that lets you live the life you imagine for yourself. What matters isn't the size of your purpose—it's whether it's genuinely yours and whether it actually motivates you when things get difficult.

> *"For a long time, I was in college because everyone said I should be. My parents, my teachers, society in general. That wasn't enough to get me through the truly hard parts when I wanted to quit. I had to find my own reason that was really mine. For me, it's about being able to help my younger siblings have more options than I did growing up. When I remember that, I can push through almost anything."*
>
> *—First-generation college student*

Sometimes purpose starts vague and becomes clearer over time through experience. That's completely normal and okay. You don't need to have your whole life figured out to have a sense of purpose that motivates you today. You might start with a general direction—'I want to help people' or 'I want to understand how things work' or 'I want to create things that matter'—and let experience sharpen that into something more specific as you learn more about yourself and the world around you.

Be wary of purposes that come entirely from outside yourself—what your parents want for you, what society says is impressive, what seems like the 'right' thing to do. These external purposes can carry you for a while, but they often run out of fuel during genuinely difficult times when you need motivation most. The purpose that sustains you through real hardship is one you've claimed for yourself, even if it was originally sparked by someone else's expectation or suggestion.

Take time to articulate your purpose clearly. Write it down somewhere you can see it. Revisit it when you're struggling and need to remember why you're doing this. Let it evolve as you grow and change and learn more about yourself. A clear sense of why you're doing this makes every other decision easier and gives meaning to the daily grind that might otherwise feel pointless and exhausting.

Making Good Decisions

College is absolutely full of decisions—what to major in, which classes to take, which opportunities to pursue, how to spend your precious time, who to spend it with, when to say yes and when to say no. For first-gen students, many of these decisions come without the guidance that other students might get from family experience and dinner table conversations. Learning to make good decisions is a skill that will serve you well long after graduation.

Start with your purpose and values as a foundation. When you know what matters most to you and why you're here, decisions become clearer and less agonizing. Does this opportunity move you toward your purpose or away from it? Does this choice align with your values or conflict with them? Using purpose as a filter helps you avoid getting pulled in too many directions at once and spreading yourself too thin.

Gather information before deciding whenever you can. Talk to people who've made similar decisions and can share what they learned. Research what different paths actually involve day to day, not just what they look like from the outside. Don't assume you know what a career, a major, or an opportunity is like based on stereotypes or surface impressions. The more accurate information you have, the better your decision will be.

> *"I thought I wanted to be a doctor because that's what successful people in my community did. That was the dream everyone talked about. Then I actually shadowed some doctors and realized it wasn't for me at all. Taking time to really explore and get information saved me from years of pursuing the wrong path. Now I'm in public health, which fits me so much better."*
>
> *—First-generation college student*

Accept that you won't have perfect information. At some point, you have to decide with what you know instead of waiting for certainty. Waiting for complete certainty often means waiting forever while opportunities pass you by. Most decisions aren't permanent anyway—you can change majors, switch careers, redirect your path based on what you learn. Making a decision and adjusting based on what you discover is usually better than staying paralyzed by indecision indefinitely.

Pay attention to how different options make you feel when you imagine pursuing them. Your gut reactions carry real wisdom, even if you can't fully explain them logically. If an opportunity looks great on paper but makes you feel drained or anxious when you actually think about pursuing it, that feeling is data worth considering seriously. If something feels right even though it's scary and uncertain, that feeling matters too.

Get advice from people you trust, but remember the decision is ultimately yours to make. Mentors, advisors, family, and friends can all offer valuable perspectives you might miss on your own. But they're not living your life day to day. They don't fully know your values, your circumstances, your specific dreams. Listen to their input, consider it seriously, and then make the decision that's right for you—even if others don't fully understand it or would have chosen differently.

Research by Schwartz and colleagues in 2021 emphasized the importance of mentoring relationships in helping students navigate decisions and see possibilities they might not have considered. Good mentors don't tell you what to do; they help you think through options and understand implications you might not see on your own. Seek out these relationships and use them wisely when facing big decisions.

Setting Goals That Matter

Goals give your purpose concrete form that you can actually work with. They turn vague aspirations into specific targets you can work toward and measure progress against. But not all goals are equally useful or motivating. Learning to set good goals—ones that actually motivate you and move you forward—is an important skill worth developing.

Good goals are specific enough to guide action clearly. 'Do better in school' is too vague to be useful—it doesn't tell you what to actually do. 'Raise my GPA to 3.0 by the end of the semester' gives you something concrete to work toward and measure. 'Build better relationships' is fuzzy and unmeasurable. 'Have a meaningful conversation with a professor every two weeks' is actionable and specific. The more specific your goal, the clearer your path to reaching it becomes.

Good goals are challenging but achievable with effort. If a goal is too easy, it won't motivate you or lead to real growth.

If it's genuinely impossible given your circumstances, you'll get discouraged and give up. The sweet spot is goals that stretch you —that require real effort and growth beyond where you are now —but that you can actually reach if you commit fully and do the work consistently.

Good goals connect to your deeper purpose in clear ways. A goal that doesn't connect to anything you actually care about at a fundamental level is hard to sustain when things get difficult. Why do you want to raise that GPA? Why does that relationship matter to you? When you can see how a specific goal serves your larger purpose, motivation comes more naturally and lasts longer.

> *"I used to set goals I thought I should have—things that looked impressive or that other people seemed to value. I almost never followed through on them because they weren't really mine at a deep level. Now I only set goals I actually care about, goals connected to who I want to become. Those are the ones I actually stick with when things get hard."*
>
> *—First-generation college student*

Research by Berzenski in 2021 found that students who set smaller, more specific goals were more likely to achieve them than students who set big, vague goals. This doesn't mean you can't have big dreams—it means you break those dreams down into concrete steps you can actually take. Each small goal achieved builds momentum and confidence toward the larger vision you're working toward.

Write your goals down and review them regularly. Goals that stay only in your head tend to fade and shift and get forgotten. Goals on paper stay concrete and hold you accountable to yourself. Check in weekly or monthly: Are you making progress? Do the goals still make sense given what you've learned? Do they need to be adjusted based on new information or changed circumstances?

Don't have too many goals competing for your attention at once. Focus is power. Three to five meaningful goals at a time is usually plenty for anyone. If you try to pursue everything simultaneously, you'll make real progress on nothing. Choose what matters most right now, give it your focused attention, and let other possibilities wait their turn.

Navigating Uncertainty

Here's something nobody tells you directly: the path forward is never as clear as it looks from the outside. Everyone is figuring it out as they go, even the people who seem to have it all together and know exactly what they're doing. Learning to navigate uncertainty—to move forward even when you can't see the whole path clearly—is essential for building a life you're genuinely proud of.

Uncertainty is uncomfortable for almost everyone. We want to know what's coming, to feel in control of our lives, to have guarantees that our choices will work out the way we hope. But that certainty rarely exists in reality, especially for first-gen students charting new territory without a map. The discomfort of uncertainty is something you learn to tolerate and work with, not something you can eliminate entirely.

One helpful reframe: instead of trying to find the 'right' path (implying there's only one correct answer), focus on making good choices with the information you have available and adjusting as you go. Life isn't about finding a predetermined destiny that's waiting for you. It's about creating a meaningful path through the choices you make day by day, year by year.

> *"I spent so much energy worrying about whether I was making the right choice, like there was one perfect answer I might miss if I wasn't careful. Eventually I realized there's no perfect answer*

—just choices with different consequences and tradeoffs. My job is to make thoughtful choices and then work hard to make them turn out well. That shift in thinking took so much pressure off."

—First-generation college student

Embrace experimentation as a way of learning. Try things. Take opportunities even when you're not completely sure they're exactly right. You learn more about what you want and what fits you through actual experience than through endless deliberation and planning. Some experiments will fail or not work out—that's fine and expected. Each one teaches you something valuable about yourself and your direction.

Build flexibility into your plans wherever you can. Don't lock yourself into paths that are extremely hard to change if things don't work out. Keep options open when you reasonably can. The world changes, you change, opportunities change in unexpected ways. Rigid plans often break under pressure; flexible plans can adapt and thrive.

Find comfort in your own growth rather than in certainty about outcomes. You're not the same person you were when you started college, and you won't be the same person when you finish. The skills, knowledge, relationships, and resilience you're building travel with you wherever you end up going. Even if specific plans don't work out the way you hoped, you're becoming someone capable of handling whatever comes next.

Permission to Dream Bigger

Many first-gen students limit their dreams without even realizing they're doing it. When you haven't seen people like you in certain spaces—in leadership positions, in graduate school, in prestigious careers, in positions of real influence—it's hard to imagine yourself there. The ceiling you can't see is still a ceiling that limits you. Part of charting your path forward is giving yourself permission to dream bigger than your current view allows.

Research by Museus and Chang in 2021 found that students with a strong sense of identity showed greater resilience and openness to possibility. Knowing who you are gives you a solid foundation for imagining who you might become. Your background isn't a limitation on your future—it's part of the unique perspective you bring to whatever you do.

Look for role models who've traveled paths similar to yours. First-gen students have gone on to become doctors, lawyers, professors, executives, entrepreneurs, artists, scientists, and leaders in every field imaginable. Their success doesn't guarantee yours, but it proves that your starting point doesn't determine your ending point. What's possible for them is genuinely possible for you too.

> *"I never thought about graduate school as a real possibility until a professor mentioned it to me directly. No one in my family had done anything like that—it just wasn't on my radar as something people like me did. But once the idea was planted in my mind, I couldn't let it go. Now I'm applying to PhD programs. It still feels surreal sometimes, but I'm doing it."*
>
> *—First-generation college student*

Challenge the assumptions you've absorbed about what people like you can achieve. Those assumptions often come from limited exposure to possibilities, not from actual reality about what's available. The world is so much bigger than your hometown or your family's experience. There are opportunities you haven't heard of yet, paths you haven't discovered, possibilities you can't currently imagine. Stay open to being surprised.

Dreaming bigger doesn't mean being unrealistic or ignoring real challenges. It means not letting fear or limited vision prematurely close doors that could lead somewhere meaningful. You can dream big and still take practical steps. You can aim high and still build the skills and relationships you need to get there. Big dreams with small consistent steps—that's how ambitious things actually get accomplished.

At the same time, success isn't only about impressive achievements or prestigious positions. A meaningful life might mean deep relationships, creative fulfillment, serving your community, raising a family well, or finding peace and contentment. Your definition of success is yours to make. Don't let anyone else's definition constrain what you're building.

Becoming Who You're Meant to Be

Throughout this book, we've talked about growth, change, and development. But there's something important to add: becoming your fullest self isn't just about acquiring skills or reaching goals or checking boxes. It's about integrating all the parts of who you are—where you came from, where you are now, and where you're going—into a coherent, authentic whole.

First-gen students sometimes feel they have to choose between their origins and their aspirations. They feel pressure to leave their old selves completely behind to fit into new environments, or to hold themselves back to avoid seeming like they're abandoning where they came from. Neither extreme serves you well or leads to a fulfilling life.

The goal isn't to become someone completely different from who you were before college. It's to become a fuller, more developed version of yourself—someone who carries their roots forward into new territory, who bridges worlds instead of abandoning one for the other. Your background isn't baggage to shed; it's perspective that enriches whatever you do and makes your contribution unique.

> *"I used to think I had to choose—be the person my family wanted or be the person college was mak-*

ing me into. I eventually realized I could be both at the same time. I can be educated and still connected to my roots. I can be ambitious and still loyal to where I came from. I don't have to split myself in two."

—First-generation college student

Research by Palmer and Maramba in 2021 highlighted how important it is for students from underrepresented backgrounds to maintain connection to their identities and communities while pursuing higher education. Success doesn't require abandoning who you are at your core. The strongest version of yourself includes all of your experience, not just the parts that fit easily into new environments.

As you move forward, keep integrating rather than fragmenting. Let your education inform your understanding of your background, and let your background inform how you use your education. Bring the wisdom of your community into new spaces that need it, and bring new knowledge back to your community that can benefit from it. Be a bridge between worlds, not someone who crossed a bridge and then burned it behind them.

Your Next Steps

So where do you go from here? This book has given you frameworks, strategies, and encouragement, but books don't change lives by themselves—actions do. The question is what you'll actually do differently starting today based on what you've learned.

Don't try to change everything at once. Pick one or two things from this book that resonated most strongly with you, and focus on those first. Maybe it's building one new habit that could make a real difference. Maybe it's having a conversation with a potential mentor. Maybe it's revisiting your sense of purpose and getting clearer about why you're here. Start where the energy is, where you feel most motivated to act.

Review this book periodically as you progress through college. Different chapters will become more relevant at different times in your journey. What you need as a freshman differs significantly from what you need as a senior facing graduation. Return to these ideas when you need them, not just once and then forget them on a shelf.

Share what you've learned with other first-gen students who could benefit. One of the most powerful things you can do with knowledge is pass it on to others. When you meet students who are struggling the way you once struggled, help them with what you know. Be the mentor you wish you'd had when you started. Your experience becomes a resource for others who come after you.

> *"The biggest gift I received in college was someone believing in me before I believed in myself. Now I try to be that person for others coming up behind me. I volunteer with incoming first-gen students, sharing what I've learned the hard way. It helps them, but honestly, it helps me too. It reminds me how far I've come."*
>
> *—First-generation college student*

Keep going even when it's hard. You now have tools and frameworks that many students don't have access to. You understand how habits work, why relationships matter so much, what resilience actually looks like in practice, and how to keep your purpose in view when daily struggles threaten to obscure it. Use these tools actively. They won't eliminate difficulty, but they'll help you navigate it more effectively than if you were figuring everything out from scratch.

Believe that you belong here and that you deserve success. Imposter syndrome will whisper that you're not enough, that you're fooling everyone, that you'll eventually be exposed as a fraud who doesn't belong. Don't believe those lies. You earned your place through real effort. You're doing the work every day. The doubt is just noise in your head—don't let it make your decisions for you.

A Final Word

College will change you. That's not a warning—it's a promise and an invitation. You'll learn things that reshape how you see the world around you. You'll grow in ways you can't predict from where you're standing now. You'll struggle and overcome and struggle again. You'll build relationships that last decades. You'll discover capabilities you didn't know you had hidden inside you.

The student you are today is not the student you'll be when you graduate, and that's exactly as it should be. Growth is the whole point of this experience. The challenges along the way aren't obstacles to the real experience—they are the real experience. They're how transformation happens.

You're writing a story that no one in your family has written before. That's scary, but it's also extraordinary. You're expanding what's possible for the people who come after you—your siblings, your future children, students from your community who will see what you accomplished and believe they can do it too. Your success ripples outward in ways you may never fully see.

So take what you've learned from this book and go make something meaningful with your education and your life. You have purpose to pursue, habits to build, relationships to nurture, resilience to strengthen, and a path to chart. None of it will be easy, but all of it will be worth it.

You learned how to stay. Now go build a life worth staying for.

What Research Helps Us Understand

Research consistently shows that students who approach

their education with a clear sense of purpose, specific and meaningful goals, and connection to their identity show stronger persistence and achievement. First-gen students who maintain ties to their backgrounds while pursuing higher education demonstrate greater resilience and life satisfaction. The skills developed in college—critical thinking, problem-solving, communication, and self-regulation—transfer broadly to life after graduation. Students who build strong support networks, develop effective habits, and cultivate resilience create foundations for success that extend far beyond their academic careers.

The Huddle

Take time to reflect on these questions thoughtfully, alone or with others.

Take time alone or with others to work through these questions. They bring together everything you've learned and point you toward your next steps.

Begin by considering this: what are the key themes from each chapter of this book? Create a brief summary of what you learned about identity, learning, habits, relationships, and resilience.

Next, reflect on this: explain in your own words how purpose, goals, and daily habits connect to each other. Why does having all three matter for success?

Take a moment to think about this: identify one specific change you want to make based on this book. What's the first small step you'll take this week to start?

Consider this honestly: look at your current life through the lens of this book. Where are you strongest? Where are the biggest gaps between where you are and where you want to be?

Now ask yourself: assess your sense of purpose honestly. Is it clear enough to guide your decisions? Is it truly yours, or does it come primarily from others' expectations?

Reflect carefully on this: write a vision statement for your life five years from now. Who do you want to be? What do you want to have accomplished? What kind of life do you want to be living?

Finally, consider this: create a commitment letter to yourself. What do you promise to do, to remember, and to believe as you continue your college journey and beyond?

Your story is still being written. Make it one worth telling.

CHAPTER 7

Preparing for Life After College

Beyond the Degree: Preparing for What Comes Next

> *"Senior year hit me hard. I'd spent so much energy figuring out how to succeed in college that I hadn't thought much about what came after. Suddenly graduation was real, and I had no idea what I was doing. I wish someone had told me earlier to start preparing for life after the degree."*
>
> *—First-generation college student*

College is not the destination. It's a launching pad. The degree you're working toward matters, but what you do with it matters even more. For first-gen students, the transition from college to career or graduate school can feel like entering yet another world with its own hidden curriculum—unwritten rules that no one explains but everyone is expected to follow.

The student who opens this chapter voices a regret that many seniors share: she focused so intensely on getting through college that she didn't prepare for what came next until it was almost too late. This is completely understandable—college demands so much attention that it's genuinely hard to think beyond the next exam or the next paper deadline. But the choices you make now, even as an underclassman, shape the options available to you when graduation arrives.

This chapter is about looking beyond the degree. We'll explore how to build experiences that open doors, how to think about career paths when you don't have family connections in professional fields, how to consider graduate school if that interests you, and how to manage the financial realities that come with adult life. By the end, you'll have a clearer picture of how to prepare for the transition ahead—not to add more stress to your plate, but to give you confidence that you're building toward something real and meaningful.

Here's the truth: first-gen students often have fewer professional connections, less exposure to different career options, and less guidance about navigating the job market or graduate school applications. But these gaps can absolutely be closed with intention and effort. The same strategies that helped you succeed in college—seeking help, building relationships, learning the hidden rules—will help you succeed in whatever comes next. You've already proven you can navigate unfamiliar territory. This is just the next territory to navigate.

Don't wait until senior year to think about this. The students who transition most smoothly are those who started preparing early—building skills, gaining experience, making connections, and exploring options while they still had time to adjust course if needed. Whatever year you're in now, this chapter will help you think strategically about what comes after graduation.

Building Experience That Matters

Your transcript tells employers and graduate schools what classes you took and what grades you earned. But that's only part of the picture they want to see. They also want to know what you've actually done—what experiences you've had, what skills you've built, what you've accomplished beyond the classroom. Building meaningful experience during college is one of the most important things you can do to prepare for what comes next.

Internships are one of the most valuable experiences you can gain during college. They give you real-world exposure to a field, help you build professional skills, connect you with potential employers, and let you test whether a career path actually fits you before you commit to it. Many jobs now expect candidates to have internship experience before they'll even consider them for entry-level positions. This is the reality of the current job market.

> *"I didn't know internships were even a thing until my junior year. No one in my family had ever done one, so it wasn't on my radar at all. By the time I started applying, a lot of my classmates already had two or three internships on their resumes. I felt so far behind. I wish I'd started looking sophomore year or even freshman year."*
>
> *—First-generation college student*

Start looking for internships earlier than you think you need to. Many programs recruit a full year in advance, especially larger companies with structured internship programs. Your campus career center can help you find opportunities and prepare your application materials. Don't assume internships are only for certain majors or certain types of students—opportunities exist across fields, and many are specifically designed for students without prior experience.

If paid internships aren't accessible to you because of financial constraints—and this is a real barrier for many first-gen students who need to work to support themselves—look for alternatives. Some internships offer stipends or housing assistance. Some can be done part-time during the school year alongside your other commitments. Research experiences with professors sometimes pay and provide similar benefits to industry internships. Campus jobs in relevant offices can build transferable skills. Be creative about finding experience that works with your financial reality.

Research by Hora and colleagues in 2021 found that internship quality matters as much as internship quantity. An internship where you do meaningful work, receive mentorship, and build real skills is worth more than one where you just make copies and fetch coffee. When evaluating opportunities, ask about what you'll actually be doing and learning day to day, not just the prestige of the company name on your resume.

> *"My research assistant position with a professor ended up being way more valuable than the fancy corporate internship my roommate had. I actually got to do real work, learn real skills, and build a relationship with someone who later wrote my strongest recommendation letter. The name on your resume matters less than what you actually learned and can talk about in interviews."*
>
> *—First-generation college student*

Beyond internships, look for other ways to build experience. Leadership roles in student organizations demonstrate that you can take initiative, work with others, and manage responsibilities. Volunteer work related to your interests shows passion and commitment. Part-time jobs build transferable skills like communication, problem-solving, and working with diverse people. Research projects develop analytical and critical thinking skills. Community engagement shows you care about more than just yourself. All of these can demonstrate to future employers or graduate programs that you're capable, motivated, and ready for the next level.

Keep track of what you accomplish in each experience. Note specific projects, achievements, and skills developed. These details will help you write compelling resumes and give concrete examples in interviews. Vague descriptions don't stand out; specific accomplishments do. Maintain a running document where you record your achievements as they happen, so you don't forget important details when it's time to apply for jobs or graduate programs.

Building Your Professional Network

You've heard it before: it's not just what you know, it's who you know. This can feel deeply unfair, especially for first-gen students whose families may not have professional connections to share. But here's the good news: you can build your own network from scratch. It takes intentional effort, but it's absolutely possible—and it's one of the most valuable things you can do for your future career.

Networking isn't about schmoozing or being fake or pretending to be someone you're not. It's about building genuine relationships with people who can help you learn, grow, and find opportunities. It's about connecting with people who've traveled paths you're interested in and learning from their experience. It's about creating a web of relationships that supports your professional development over time.

Start with the people around you right now. Professors who teach in your field of interest. Supervisors from jobs or internships. Alumni who've graduated from your program. Guest speakers who visit your classes. Staff members in offices related to your goals. These people are accessible to you now, and many of them genuinely want to help students succeed. You just have to reach out and make the connection.

> *"I was terrified of networking because I thought it meant going to fancy events and making awkward small talk with strangers in business suits. Then I realized I was already networking—I just didn't call it that. Every time I talked to a professor about my career interests or asked an alum about their job, I was building my network. It felt much less scary when I saw it that way."*
>
> *—First-generation college student*

LinkedIn is a powerful tool for professional networking that costs nothing to use. Create a profile that highlights your education, experience, and skills. Connect with people you meet professionally. Follow companies and organizations you're interested in. Many professionals are willing to have informational conversations with students who reach out respectfully—this is a great way to learn about career paths and make connections that might help you later.

When you reach out to someone for networking purposes, be specific about why you're contacting them and what you're asking for. 'I'm a junior studying biology and I'm interested in public health careers. I saw you work at the health department. Would you be willing to have a fifteen-minute phone call to tell me about your career path?' This kind of specific, respectful request usually gets much better responses than vague ones that don't explain what you want.

Research by Smith and colleagues in 2022 emphasized that social capital—the networks and relationships that provide access to opportunities—significantly impacts career outcomes. First-gen students may start with less social capital, but they can build it through intentional networking efforts. The relationships you develop now can open doors for decades to come.

> *"A connection I made at a campus career fair led to my first job after graduation. The recruiter remembered me because I'd asked thoughtful questions and followed up with a thank-you email afterward. When a position opened up six months later, she thought of me. That one interaction at a career fair changed my whole career trajectory."*
>
> *—First-generation college student*

Your network isn't just for finding jobs—though it definitely helps with that. It's also for getting advice, learning about industries, finding mentors, and staying connected to opportunities throughout your career. Invest in these relationships genuinely, not just transactionally when you need something, and they'll pay dividends for years.

Remember to maintain relationships over time. Check in with people occasionally even when you don't need anything. Share updates about your progress. Congratulate them on their achievements. Networking is about building real relationships, not just collecting business cards or LinkedIn connections.

Considering Graduate School

For some careers, a bachelor's degree is just the beginning. Medicine, law, academia, many scientific fields, and some other professions require graduate or professional education. For other careers, an advanced degree isn't required but can open doors to higher-level positions. Understanding whether graduate school makes sense for your goals is an important part of planning your path forward.

Graduate school is a significant investment of time, energy, and often money. A master's degree typically takes one to two years of full-time study. A PhD can take five to seven years or even more depending on the field. Professional degrees like law or medicine have their own timelines and requirements. Before committing to this path, you need to understand what you're getting into and whether it's truly necessary for your goals.

Start by researching what credentials are actually required or valued in the field you're interested in. Talk to people working in that field at various levels. Some careers truly require advanced degrees—you can't be a licensed physician without medical school, for example. Others value them but don't require them. Still others don't care much about graduate education at all and value experience more. Don't assume you need a graduate degree without investigating whether that's actually true for your specific goals.

> *"I assumed I needed a master's degree to get anywhere in my field. Then I talked to some professionals and learned that experience mattered*

way more than credentials for the jobs I actually wanted. I decided to work for a few years first, and now my employer is paying for my graduate degree. I saved a lot of money and gained valuable experience by not rushing into grad school right away."

—First-generation college student

If graduate school does make sense for your goals, start preparing early. Many programs look for specific prerequisites, research experience, strong faculty recommendations, and competitive test scores. Building these qualifications takes time—often years, not months. Talk to advisors in your field about what strong applicants look like and what you should be doing to prepare.

Funding is a major consideration, especially for first-gen students who may not have family resources to fall back on. Many PhD programs are fully funded—they pay you a stipend and cover your tuition in exchange for research or teaching work. Master's programs are more variable, with some offering funding and others expecting you to pay significant tuition. Professional schools like law and medicine typically require significant loans. Understand the financial implications before you commit.

Research by Roksa and colleagues in 2022 found that first-gen students are underrepresented in graduate education, particularly in doctoral programs. This isn't because first-gen students are less capable—it's because they often have less exposure to graduate school as a realistic option and less guidance about how to get there. If graduate school interests you, seek out mentors and resources that can help you navigate the process successfully.

"I didn't know PhD programs paid you until a professor told me junior year. I'd always thought

grad school was for rich kids who could afford more tuition. Learning that I could actually get paid to do research changed everything. Now I'm in a fully funded doctoral program, and I've never had to pay a dime for tuition."

—First-generation college student

Don't rule out graduate school just because no one in your family has done it. But also don't pursue it just because it seems like the next logical step. Make an informed decision based on your actual career goals, the realities of the programs and job markets in your field, and your personal and financial situation.

Navigating the Job Search

For students heading into the job market after graduation, the search process can feel overwhelming—especially if you don't have family members who've navigated professional hiring before. Understanding how the process works demystifies it and helps you approach it strategically rather than randomly applying everywhere and hoping for the best.

Start earlier than you think you need to. Many employers recruit for post-graduation positions six months to a year in advance. Some industries, like consulting and investment banking, have recruiting timelines that begin even earlier. If you wait until spring of senior year to start looking, you may have already missed important deadlines. Pay attention to recruiting timelines in your field and plan accordingly.

Your campus career center is one of your most valuable resources. They can help you write resumes and cover letters, practice interviewing, find job postings, and connect with employers who actively recruit from your school. Many students don't use these services until they're desperate, but the students who use them early and often have a significant advantage.

"I went to the career center every other week

starting junior year. They reviewed my resume probably ten times, helped me prep for every interview, and connected me with alumni in my field. By the time I was seriously job hunting, I knew exactly what I was doing. My friends who never went there were scrambling and stressed."

—First-generation college student

Your resume should highlight not just your education but your experiences, skills, and accomplishments. Use specific examples and quantify results when possible. 'Increased social media engagement by 40 percent' is more compelling than 'managed social media accounts.' Tailor your resume to each position, emphasizing the qualifications that match what the employer is looking for. One generic resume for all applications rarely works as well as customized versions.

Interviews can be intimidating, but they're a skill you can practice and improve. Research common interview questions in your field. Practice your answers out loud—actually saying them, not just thinking them in your head. Do mock interviews with career counselors, friends, or mentors. The more you practice, the more comfortable and confident you'll be when the real interview comes.

Be prepared for rejection. Even strong candidates get rejected from many jobs before landing one. This doesn't mean something is wrong with you—it's just how competitive job markets work. Each rejection teaches you something and brings you closer to the right opportunity. Don't take it personally, and don't let it stop you from continuing to apply.

"I applied to over fifty jobs and got rejected from most of them. It was discouraging, but I kept going. Eventually I got three offers and was able to choose the best one. If I'd given up after the first twenty rejections, I never would have found

> *the job I love now."*
>
> *—First-generation college student*

Salary negotiation is another area where first-gen students often have less preparation. Research typical salaries for the positions you're applying to so you know what's reasonable to expect. When you receive an offer, it's usually acceptable to negotiate—but do your homework first and approach it professionally. Career counselors can help you prepare for these conversations.

Financial Literacy for the Real World

Managing money as a working adult is different from managing money as a student. You'll likely have a regular income for the first time, but also new expenses and responsibilities that may surprise you. Understanding basic financial principles now will help you build a stable foundation for your adult life and avoid common mistakes that can set you back for years.

If you took out student loans, understand your repayment obligations before you graduate. Know how much you owe in total, what your monthly payments will be, and when they start. Research income-driven repayment plans that can make payments more manageable if your starting salary is modest. Don't ignore your loans—they won't go away, and defaulting has serious consequences for your credit and your future.

> *"I graduated with no idea what I actually owed or when I had to start paying it back. When the bills came, I panicked. I wish I'd paid more attention to the financial literacy workshops they offered. Now I tell every undergrad I meet to actually go to those things."*
>
> *—First-generation college student*

Build a budget that accounts for your actual expenses. Rent, utilities, food, transportation, insurance, loan payments, and basic needs add up faster than most new graduates expect. Use a budgeting app or spreadsheet to track where your money goes each month. Living within your means from the start prevents debt from piling up.

Start saving early, even if it's just a small amount. An emergency fund of three to six months of expenses protects you from unexpected setbacks like job loss or medical bills. If your employer offers a retirement plan with matching contributions, contribute at least enough to get the full match—that's essentially free money for your future.

Be cautious with credit. Credit cards can be useful tools for building credit history and managing cash flow, but they can also lead to high-interest debt if you spend more than you can pay off each month. Understand how interest works, pay your balance in full when possible, and don't let lifestyle inflation eat up your income as you earn more.

Research by Lusardi and Mitchell in 2023 found that financial literacy significantly impacts long-term financial wellbeing. Students who learn basic money management skills before entering the workforce make better decisions and build wealth more effectively over time. This knowledge may not have been taught in your family, but you can learn it now and break cycles of financial struggle.

> *"Nobody in my family ever talked about retirement accounts or investing. I learned about compound interest in a personal finance workshop, and it blew my mind. Starting to save in my twenties instead of my forties will literally be worth hundreds of thousands of dollars by the time I retire. I wish everyone knew this."*
>
> *—First-generation college student*

Paying It Forward After Graduation

As you move beyond college and into your career, you'll have opportunities and perspectives that many people in your community may not have had. Part of building a meaningful life is finding ways to give back—to help others who are traveling paths similar to yours, to use your success to create opportunities for those coming behind you.

Mentoring other first-gen students is one of the most impactful things you can do. Your experience navigating college and career transitions gives you wisdom that can help others avoid pitfalls and find opportunities. Even as a recent graduate, you have knowledge that current students desperately need. Volunteer with first-gen programs at your alma mater or in your community.

When you're in a position to hire or influence hiring decisions, remember what it was like to not have connections. Give opportunities to candidates from non-traditional backgrounds who might be overlooked by people who only hire from their own networks. Be the door-opener for others that you wished you had when you were starting out.

> *"A first-gen alum took a chance on me for my first internship when I had no experience and no connections. Now that I'm in a position to hire interns myself, I do the same thing. I specifically look for students who remind me of myself—hungry, hardworking, but without the advantages that make breaking in easier."*
>
> *—First-generation college student*

Your success challenges narratives about what people from your background can achieve. By succeeding visibly, you expand what seems possible for others. Your younger siblings, cousins, neighbors, and community members see what you've accomplished and realize that they might be able to do it too. Never underestimate the power of your example.

Starting Now, Wherever You Are

Regardless of what year you're in, there are things you can do now to prepare for what comes after graduation. The earlier you start, the more options you'll have when the time comes to make decisions about your future.

If you're a freshman or sophomore, focus on exploration. Try different courses, activities, and experiences to discover what genuinely interests you. Build relationships with professors who can guide you. Start thinking about potential majors and careers without locking yourself in too early. Look into what internships or research opportunities might be available to you.

If you're a junior, get serious about building experience. Apply for internships and research positions. Develop relationships with mentors who can guide and recommend you. Research career paths and graduate school options that interest you. Start building your professional network intentionally.

If you're a senior, execute your plan. Apply for jobs or graduate programs. Use every resource your campus offers. Prepare thoroughly for interviews and applications. Connect with alumni and professionals in your field. Don't wait—timelines move faster than you expect.

> *"Every year I wished I'd started preparing earlier. As a freshman, I wished I'd done more in high school. As a junior, I wished I'd explored more as a sophomore. As a senior, I wished I'd gained more experience as a junior. The lesson I finally learned: whatever year you're in, start now. Future you will thank present you."*
>
> *—First-generation college student*

The skills you've developed through this book—understanding yourself, building habits, nurturing relationships, cultivating resilience, clarifying purpose—all transfer directly to life after college. The same approaches that helped you succeed as a student will help you succeed as a professional. You're not starting from scratch; you're building on a foundation you've already laid.

The transition beyond college is another navigation challenge, similar to the one you faced coming into college. You've already proven you can navigate unfamiliar territory. You can learn new rules, build new relationships, and find your way in new environments. Trust yourself. You've done hard things before. You can do this too.

What Research Helps Us Understand

Research on post-college transitions shows that students who gain meaningful experience during college—through internships, research, and leadership—have stronger employment outcomes and smoother transitions to professional life. First-gen students benefit significantly from mentoring and networking that helps them access opportunities and navigate professional environments. Financial literacy education improves long-term financial wellbeing. Graduate school pathways become more accessible when students receive guidance about the application process and funding opportunities. The skills developed in college—critical thinking, communication, relationship-building, and resilience—transfer directly to professional success.

The Huddle

Take time to reflect on these questions thoughtfully, alone or with others.

Take time alone or with others to work through these questions. They help you prepare practically for what comes after graduation.

Begin by considering this: list the main types of experience-building opportunities discussed in this chapter. Which ones have you already pursued? Which ones should you explore?

Next, reflect on this: explain in your own words why networking matters for career success. How can first-gen students build professional networks even without family connections?

Take a moment to think about this: identify one specific action you can take this semester to build experience or connections for your future. When will you do it?

Consider this honestly: research the typical career paths in a field that interests you. What experience, credentials, and connections do people in that field usually have? What gaps do you need to fill?

Now ask yourself: assess your current financial literacy. What do you understand well? What do you need to learn more about before graduation?

Reflect carefully on this: draft a timeline for your remaining time in college. What do you want to accomplish each semester to prepare for life after graduation?

Finally, consider this: write a letter to a future first-gen student who will be in your position someday. What advice would you give them about preparing for life beyond the degree?

The degree opens doors. What you build through those doors is up to you. As you reflect on these questions, remember that career preparation is not something that happens in your final semester. It is something you build incrementally through every experience, every relationship, and every skill you develop throughout your college years. The students who transition most successfully into professional life are not necessarily those with the highest grades or the most prestigious internships. They are the ones who approached college with intentionality, who sought out experiences that stretched them beyond their comfort zone, and who built genuine relationships with mentors and peers who could support their growth. Your first-generation background gives you a unique advantage in the professional world. The resilience, adaptability, and resourcefulness you developed navigating unfamiliar systems in college are exactly the qualities employers value most. You have already proven you can learn quickly, persist through difficulty, and advocate for yourself in spaces that were not designed for you. Those are not just survival skills. They are leadership qualities. As you move forward, trust the foundation you have built and give yourself permission to pursue opportunities that excite you, even if they seem beyond your reach. The person who showed up on the first day of college and the person you are now are fundamentally different, and the person you will become in the years ahead will continue to grow in ways you cannot yet imagine.

CHAPTER 8

Navigating Challenges and Staying the Course

Navigating the Practical Side: Money, Health, and Campus Resources

> *"Nobody told me that college would be as much about surviving the system as surviving the classes. Learning where to go when I was broke, sick, or confused about paperwork—that knowledge saved me as much as any study strategy ever did."*
>
> *—First-generation college student*

We've spent seven chapters talking about the internal work of college success—building identity, developing habits, forming relationships, cultivating resilience, clarifying purpose, and understanding your legacy. All of that matters deeply and forms the foundation of your success. But there's another side to the college experience that can make or break your success: the practical, everyday challenges of navigating systems, managing money, taking care of your health, and knowing where to go when you need help with something specific.

The student who opens this chapter names a truth that many first-gen students discover through hard experience: surviving the system is its own challenge, completely separate from surviving the academics. You can have perfect study habits and still get derailed by a financial aid crisis that threatens your enrollment. You can have strong relationships and still struggle when your health falls apart and you can't keep up. You can have clear purpose and still get lost in bureaucratic mazes that nobody ever explained to you.

This chapter is about the practical side of college success—

the nuts and bolts of navigating systems that weren't designed with first-gen students in mind. We'll cover financial literacy and managing the stress that comes with money worries, taking care of your physical and mental health in a demanding environment, and understanding how to actually use the campus resources that exist specifically to help you. This is the hidden curriculum made visible and practical.

For first-gen students, these practical challenges often hit harder than they do for students whose families can guide them through or cushion the blow when things go wrong. When you don't have a parent who can explain how financial aid appeals work or cover an unexpected expense with a quick transfer, every practical problem feels more threatening to your entire college career. That's why mastering this practical side isn't optional—it's essential for your survival and success.

Think of this chapter as your practical survival guide. The strategies and mindsets from earlier chapters give you the internal foundation. This chapter gives you the specific knowledge to navigate the external systems you'll encounter every day of your college experience.

Understanding Money in College

Let's talk about money—a topic that causes enormous stress for many first-gen students but rarely gets addressed directly in college orientation or advising sessions. Financial stress doesn't just affect your bank account. Research shows it impacts your mental health, your academic performance, your ability to focus in class, and your likelihood of persisting to graduation. Understanding how money works in college is genuinely a survival skill.

Research by Goldrick-Rab and colleagues in 2021 documented the widespread financial insecurity among college students, with many struggling to afford basic needs like food and housing even while enrolled full-time. First-gen students are disproportionately affected by these challenges. The stress of worrying about money constantly takes a real toll on everything else you're trying to accomplish academically and personally.

> *"My first semester, I was so stressed about money that I couldn't focus on anything else. I was working twenty-five hours a week on top of full-time classes, skipping meals to save money, and lying awake at night doing mental math about whether I could afford next semester's books. My grades suffered because my brain was always somewhere else—worrying about bills instead of focusing on what the professor was saying."*
>
> *—First-generation college student*

The first step is understanding your actual financial situation clearly, even if that feels scary. Many students avoid looking closely at their finances because it's frightening to confront, but that avoidance usually makes things worse over time. Know exactly what your tuition and fees cost each semester. Know what financial aid you're receiving and what forms it takes—grants that don't need to be repaid versus loans that do. Know what you're expected to pay out of pocket and when those payments are due. Know your monthly expenses for housing, food, transportation, books, and other necessities. You can't manage what you don't understand clearly.

Financial aid is complicated, and the financial aid office is one of the most important relationships you'll build on campus. Don't wait until there's a crisis to visit them for the first time. Go early in each semester to make sure everything is in order with your aid package. Ask questions when you don't understand something—the terminology can be genuinely confusing even for adults with college experience, so it's okay to need things explained. These staff members want to help you succeed, but they can only help if you show up and communicate with them.

Many students don't realize that financial aid packages can

sometimes be appealed or adjusted. If your family's financial situation has changed significantly since you filed your FAFSA—a job loss, a medical emergency, a divorce—you may be able to request a professional judgment review. This can result in increased aid. But you have to ask and provide documentation. The financial aid office won't know your circumstances changed unless you tell them.

> *"When my dad got laid off during my sophomore year, I thought I'd have to drop out because we couldn't afford my contribution anymore. My advisor told me to go to financial aid and explain the situation. I brought documentation of my dad's job loss, and they did something called a 'professional judgment appeal.' My aid increased by several thousand dollars. I had no idea that was even possible until someone told me."*
>
> *—First-generation college student*

Emergency funds exist on most campuses for students facing unexpected financial crises—a car repair, a medical bill, an unexpected travel expense for a family emergency. Many students don't know about these resources or feel too embarrassed to ask for help. Don't let pride prevent you from accessing money that exists specifically to help students in situations like yours. A small emergency grant of a few hundred dollars can literally be the difference between staying enrolled and having to drop out.

Be strategic about working while in school if you need to work to afford college. Many first-gen students need to work, and that's a reality that shouldn't be shamed or apologized for. But research consistently shows that working more than fifteen to twenty hours per week starts to negatively impact academic performance. If possible, try to find work that's on campus, flexible around your class schedule, and ideally connected to your career interests or major. Work-study positions often fit these criteria and may offer additional benefits.

Build basic money management skills if you don't already have them. Track your spending for a month so you know where your money actually goes—the results often surprise people. Create a simple budget that accounts for your income and essential expenses first. Build a small emergency fund if you can, even if it's just fifty or a hundred dollars—having any cushion at all reduces financial stress significantly. These aren't complicated skills, but nobody teaches them in most high schools or colleges.

> *"I started tracking every dollar I spent for a month, and I was shocked. I was spending way more on coffee and snacks than I realized—money that could have gone to textbooks or savings. Just seeing where my money went helped me make better choices without feeling deprived. Small changes added up to real savings."*
>
> *—First-generation college student*

Taking Care of Your Health

Your physical and mental health are the foundation everything else rests on. When your health suffers, everything else suffers too—your energy levels, your ability to focus, your mood and motivation, your relationships, your academic performance. Taking care of yourself isn't selfish or a luxury you can't afford. It's necessary for your success and your ability to help others over the long term.

Many first-gen students come from backgrounds where healthcare wasn't easily accessible or where mental health wasn't talked about openly or treated as legitimate. You might not be used to thinking about preventive care or asking for help when something feels wrong with your body or your mind. College is actually a good time to develop these habits because you have access to resources that you might not have later in life, and the demands on you are high enough that you can't afford to neglect your health.

Most colleges have health centers that provide basic medical care at low or no cost to enrolled students. Use them. Get your flu shot each fall. Go when you're sick instead of trying to tough it out and hope it passes. Address small health problems before they become big ones that cost more and take you out of commission longer. The health center staff are there to help you, and using their services is part of what your tuition and fees pay for.

> *"I ignored a bad cold for weeks because I didn't want to miss class and I didn't know the health center was basically free to use. By the time I finally went, it had turned into bronchitis and I ended up missing two weeks of class anyway—way more than if I'd just gone early. Now I go at the first sign of being sick. It's so much smarter to deal with things early before they get worse."*
>
> *—First-generation college student*

Mental health matters as much as physical health, even though our culture sometimes treats it as less important or less real. College is genuinely stressful, and it's completely normal to struggle sometimes with that stress. Anxiety, depression, loneliness, and feeling overwhelmed are extremely common among college students. These aren't signs of weakness or personal failure—they're signs that you're human and dealing with real challenges in a demanding environment.

Most campuses have counseling centers that provide mental health services to students. These services are usually free or very low cost as part of your enrollment. Going to counseling isn't only for people in crisis or people with diagnosed mental illness—it's also for people who want support managing everyday stress, working through difficult emotions, navigating relationship problems, or developing better coping skills. Think of it as mental health maintenance, like going to the gym for your mind.

Research by Lipson and colleagues in 2022 found that college students' mental health has declined significantly in recent years, with high rates of anxiety, depression, and other challenges across all types of institutions. At the same time, stigma around seeking mental health help has decreased substantially. More students than ever are using counseling services and talking openly about mental health. You won't be alone or unusual if you decide to go.

> *"I was raised to believe that therapy was for 'crazy people' and that strong people handle their problems themselves without complaining. When I finally went to the counseling center during a really dark time sophomore year, I realized how wrong those beliefs were. Counseling gave me tools to manage my anxiety that I still use every single day. I wish I'd gone sooner instead of suffering alone for so long."*
>
> *—First-generation college student*

Sleep, nutrition, and exercise form the physical foundation of your mental health and cognitive function. When you're not sleeping enough, eating poorly, or never moving your body, everything feels harder—including managing stress, staying motivated, focusing in class, and remembering what you study. These basics aren't luxuries or nice-to-haves. They're necessities that make everything else possible. Protect them even when you're busy, especially when you're busy.

Know the warning signs that suggest you need professional help rather than just self-care strategies: persistent sadness lasting more than two weeks, anxiety that interferes with your ability to function day to day, thoughts of self-harm or suicide, significant changes in sleep or appetite, feeling hopeless about the future, or using substances to cope with difficult feelings. If you notice these signs in yourself, reach out to the counseling center or health services. Don't wait for things to get worse.

Knowing Where to Go for What

Colleges have dozens of offices, services, and resources designed to help students succeed in various ways. The problem for many first-gen students is that nobody explains what these resources are, what they actually do, or how to use them effectively. Knowing where to go for what kind of help is a practical skill that can save you enormous time, stress, and potential derailment from your academic path.

The academic advising office helps you plan your course schedule, understand degree requirements, explore potential majors, and navigate academic policies like add/drop periods, withdrawal procedures, and academic standing. Your academic advisor should be one of the first people you build a relationship with on campus. They can help you make smart decisions about your academic path and catch problems before they become serious enough to threaten your progress.

The financial aid office handles everything related to paying for college—scholarships, grants, loans, work-study, payment plans, and appeals. If you have any questions about money and college, this is where to start. Go at least once per semester, early in the semester, to make sure your aid is in order and to learn about additional opportunities you might qualify for that you don't know about yet.

> *"I didn't know there were extra scholarships I could apply for after I was already enrolled. I just assumed whatever aid I got initially was all that existed for me. Then my advisor told me about departmental scholarships in my major that most students never applied for. I applied and got one. That was an extra two thousand dollars per year I almost missed simply because I didn't know to ask about it."*

—First-generation college student

The tutoring center or learning center provides academic support—tutoring in specific subjects, study skills workshops, and sometimes supplemental instruction for particularly difficult courses. These services are usually completely free and used by students at all levels, not just those who are struggling or failing. Smart students use tutoring proactively to do better, not just reactively to survive.

The writing center helps with any kind of writing assignment at any stage of the process, from brainstorming ideas to organizing your argument to final editing and polishing. They don't write your papers for you, but they help you become a better writer by asking questions and offering feedback. Using the writing center is not a sign of weakness—it's a sign of wisdom about how writing actually improves. Even professional writers use editors.

The career center helps you explore career paths, prepare for job and internship searches, build your resume, write cover letters, and practice interviewing skills. Don't wait until senior year to discover this resource exists. Start early and use it throughout your college career. Career exploration during your first and second years can also help you make better decisions about your major and coursework.

The Dean of Students office handles a wide range of student issues, including emergencies, conflicts, academic concerns, and situations where you're not sure who else to ask. If you're facing a crisis and don't know where to turn or which office can help, the Dean of Students office is often a good starting point. They can assess your situation and direct you to the right resource.

> *"When my mother got very sick and I had to go home for two weeks in the middle of the semester, I had no idea what to do about my classes or my grades. Someone told me to go to the Dean of Stu-*

dents office. They helped me communicate with all my professors at once, arrange to make up work, and even connected me with counseling to deal with the emotional stress. I didn't know they did all that until I needed it."

—First-generation college student

Disability services provides accommodations for students with documented disabilities—extra time on tests, note-taking assistance, accessible formats for materials, quiet testing environments, and other supports. If you have a learning disability, mental health condition, physical disability, or chronic illness that affects your academics, register with this office. The accommodations exist to level the playing field so you can show what you actually know, not to give you an unfair advantage over other students.

First-gen student programs, if your campus has one, specifically support students like you who are the first in their families to attend college. They often provide mentoring, community events, specialized advising, and resources tailored to the unique challenges first-gen students face. If this resource exists on your campus, connect with it. Being around other first-gen students who truly understand your experience can be incredibly valuable.

Surviving the Bureaucracy

College involves a lot of paperwork, deadlines, forms, and administrative processes that can feel overwhelming—especially if you're the first in your family to navigate them and don't have anyone at home to explain how things work. Learning to handle bureaucracy effectively is a practical survival skill that will serve you well beyond college in almost any career or life situation.

Keep track of important deadlines religiously. Financial aid deadlines, registration deadlines, add/drop deadlines, scholarship application deadlines, graduation application deadlines—

missing these can have serious consequences that are sometimes impossible to undo. Use a calendar or planner to record every deadline as soon as you learn about it. Set reminders a week before and again a day before deadlines approach so you're never scrambling at the last minute.

Read your official email regularly. Your college communicates important information through your student email account. Bills, registration holds, financial aid updates, required forms, opportunities, and warnings—all of these come through email. Check it at least once daily, ideally in the morning. Missing an important email because you didn't check can create problems that are very hard to undo.

> *"I almost got dropped from my classes because I didn't see an email about a hold on my account. There was a form I needed to fill out, and I had ten days to do it. I found the email on day nine, completely by accident when I was looking for something else. Now I check my student email every single morning before I do anything else, like brushing my teeth."*
>
> *—First-generation college student*

When you need something from an office, be clear about what you're asking for and persistent in following up until you get it. Bureaucracies move slowly, and things fall through the cracks even when everyone has good intentions. If someone says they'll get back to you by a certain date, note that date and follow up if they don't. Being politely persistent often gets results when passive waiting doesn't.

Keep records of important interactions and documents. Save emails, take notes on conversations including names and dates, keep copies of every form you submit. If there's ever a dispute about what was said or done, having records protects you. This is especially important for anything involving money or academic standing.

Learn to advocate for yourself in bureaucratic systems. If a policy doesn't make sense or seems unfair in your particular situation, ask questions about why it exists. Request exceptions when you have legitimate reasons. Talk to supervisors if front-line staff can't help you. Being a self-advocate doesn't mean being aggressive or rude—it means being informed, clear, and persistent about what you need.

Research by Toutkoushian and colleagues in 2021 noted that first-gen students often lack the institutional knowledge and cultural capital that helps other students navigate college systems smoothly. Building this knowledge intentionally—by asking questions, using resources, and learning from experience—closes that gap over time.

When Things Go Wrong

Despite your best efforts at preparation and prevention, practical crises will happen during your college career. Your financial aid gets messed up due to an administrative error. You get seriously sick at the worst possible time during finals. A family emergency pulls you away from school unexpectedly. The question isn't whether difficulties will occur—it's how you respond effectively when they do.

Act quickly when problems arise. Many practical problems get worse with time if ignored. A small financial aid issue becomes a big one if you ignore it for weeks. A health problem that could be treated easily becomes serious if you delay seeking help. Address problems as soon as you become aware of them, even if it feels uncomfortable or you're not sure what to do first.

Communicate with people who need to know about your situation. If something is affecting your ability to attend class or complete work, tell your professors early rather than at the last minute or after the fact. If a financial issue threatens your enrollment, talk to financial aid immediately. If a personal crisis is overwhelming you, connect with the Dean of Students. People can only help if they know you need help.

> *"When my dad lost his job suddenly, I was terrified that my financial aid wouldn't cover the difference and I'd have to drop out immediately. I almost didn't tell anyone because I was ashamed of my family's situation. But I finally went to financial aid, and they helped me file an appeal based on changed family circumstances. My aid actually increased significantly. If I'd stayed silent out of shame, I would have lost everything I'd worked for."*
>
> *—First-generation college student*

Know that most problems have solutions, even if you can't see them immediately from where you're standing. Colleges have dealt with every kind of student crisis imaginable over the years. There are usually policies, resources, or exceptions that can help—but you have to ask for them. Don't assume a problem is unsolvable before you've explored all your options with people who know the system.

Use your support network during practical crises. This is when those relationships you've built earlier become lifelines that can save your college career. A mentor might know exactly who to talk to. A friend might have dealt with something similar and can share what worked. An advisor might know about resources you don't. You don't have to figure out crisis response alone. One of the most important insights from research on student persistence is that the students who succeed are not the ones who face fewer challenges. They are the ones who develop effective responses to the challenges they face.

Every setback you navigate teaches you something about your own resilience that you could not learn any other way. Every time you reach out for support instead of withdrawing into isolation, you strengthen the network that will sustain you through future difficulties. Every time you reframe a failure as a learning opportunity rather than evidence of your inadequacy, you build the mindset that separates students who persist from those who give up. The journey you are on is not easy, but it is building something in you that will matter long after college ends. The grit, the adaptability, the emotional intelligence, and the problem-solving skills you are developing right now are not just helping you survive college. They are preparing you for a life of purpose and impact that your challenges, rather than your comfort, have made possible.

Research by Rehr and colleagues in 2021 emphasized that coping strategies make a significant difference in how students navigate challenges. Students who face problems directly, seek help early, and use available resources show substantially better outcomes than those who avoid, delay, or try to handle everything completely alone.

What Research Helps Us Understand

Research shows that practical challenges—financial stress, health problems, and difficulty navigating institutional systems—contribute significantly to student attrition, particularly among first-gen students. Financial insecurity affects mental health and academic performance in measurable ways. Students who actively use campus resources show better outcomes than those who don't. Early intervention when problems arise leads to better results than waiting until crisis point. Building practical knowledge about how college systems work is a learnable skill that improves with experience and intentional effort.

Students who develop multiple coping strategies and maintain active support networks demonstrate significantly higher persistence rates than those who rely on a single approach. The research also emphasizes the importance of institutional support structures, including counseling services, mentoring programs, and peer support groups, in creating environments where struggling students can access help without stigma.

For first-generation students specifically, the combination of strong social connections, access to institutional resources, and a growth-oriented mindset creates a resilience framework that sustains engagement even during the most challenging periods of the college experience.

The Huddle

Take time to reflect on these questions thoughtfully, alone or with others.

Take time alone or with others to work through these questions. They help you assess and strengthen your practical navigation skills.

Begin by considering this: list at least five campus resources discussed in this chapter. What does each one help with?

Next, reflect on this: explain why financial stress affects more than just your bank account. How does money worry impact academic performance and overall wellbeing?

Take a moment to think about this: identify one campus resource you haven't used yet but should. What's your specific plan to connect with that resource this semester?

Consider this honestly: think about a practical challenge you've faced in college. What did you do well in handling it? What could you have done differently knowing what you know now?

Now ask yourself: assess your current systems for managing practical matters—finances, health, deadlines, paperwork. What's working well? What needs improvement?

Reflect carefully on this: create a personal resource map. Who do you contact for financial issues? Health issues? Academic problems? Personal crises? Build a list with specific names, offices, and contact information.

Finally, consider this: design a crisis response plan. If something major went wrong next week—financial, health, family—

what would your first three steps be? Who would you contact first? The challenges you face are real and significant, but they are not permanent. Every obstacle you overcome adds another layer to the foundation of resilience you are building. The students who look back on their college years with the greatest sense of accomplishment are rarely the ones who had the easiest path. They are the ones who faced genuine difficulty and found a way through it. Your struggle is not a sign that you do not belong here. It is evidence that you are doing something genuinely hard, and doing hard things is exactly how growth happens.

Mastering the practical side of college frees your energy for what matters most—learning, growing, and building the future you're working toward. Take your time with these reflections. The challenges discussed in this chapter are not hypothetical scenarios. They are the real, daily experiences of students who are balancing academic demands with financial pressures, family responsibilities, and the emotional weight of being the first in their families to pursue a college degree. If you recognized yourself in any of these descriptions, that recognition is itself a form of strength. It means you are aware of what you are carrying, and awareness is the first step toward building the support systems that will help you carry it sustainably.

CHAPTER 9

Your Year-by-Year Roadmap

Your Journey Year by Year: Navigating Each Stage of College

> *"Every year felt completely different. Freshman year was about survival. Sophomore year was about figuring out who I really was. Junior year was about getting serious about my future. Senior year was about finishing strong and preparing for what comes next. If I'd known what to expect at each stage, I would have been so much better prepared."*
>
> *—First-generation college student*

College isn't one uniform experience that stays the same from beginning to end—it's a journey with distinct stages, each bringing its own challenges, opportunities, and developmental tasks. What you need as a first-semester freshman feeling lost and overwhelmed is very different from what you need as a graduating senior preparing to launch into the world. Understanding what's coming at each stage helps you prepare mentally, set appropriate expectations, and make the most of where you are right now.

The student who opens this chapter captures something important that many students only realize in hindsight: each year of college feels different because it genuinely is different. The challenges shift, the stakes change, and what success looks like evolves as you move through your college career. Students who understand these stages can navigate them more intentionally instead of being constantly surprised or overwhelmed by each new phase.

This chapter walks you through the four years of a typical college experience—or however many years your particular path takes—highlighting the key challenges and opportunities at each stage. Whether you're just starting out as a brand new freshman or already midway through your journey, understanding the full arc helps you see where you are, where you're going, and what you need to focus on right now.

For first-gen students, this roadmap is especially valuable because you likely don't have family members who can tell you what to expect at each stage based on their own experience walking this path before you. You're navigating without a map that others might take for granted because they heard stories about college around the dinner table their whole lives. This chapter aims to provide that map so you can move through each stage with greater confidence and intention.

Keep in mind that everyone's timeline is different, and that's perfectly okay. You might take five or six years instead of four due to various circumstances. You might transfer from a community college or another institution. You might take time off and return later. You might be balancing school with significant work or family responsibilities. The stages I describe still apply—they're developmental, not strictly chronological. Read this chapter looking for where you are in your journey, not just which calendar year you're technically in.

First Year: Building Your Foundation

The first year of college is primarily about survival and adjustment. Everything is new—the environment, the academic expectations, the people, the systems and bureaucracies. Your main job during this year is to figure out how things work, establish basic habits and routines that will support your success, and build the foundation that will support everything that comes later. If you do nothing else your first year, focus on these fundamentals.

Research consistently shows that the first year is the highest-risk period for dropping out of college. More students leave during or after their first year than at any other time in their college careers. This isn't because first-year students are weak or uncommitted—it's because the transition is genuinely hard, especially for first-gen students who are navigating completely unfamiliar territory without family guidance to fall back on.

Academically, focus on learning how to learn at the college level. High school study habits often don't work in college because the expectations are completely different, and discovering this through failed exams is painful and discouraging. Invest time early in developing effective study strategies—the ones we discussed in detail in Chapter 2. Use tutoring and other academic support services before you're in crisis, not after things have already gone badly.

> *"My first semester was a complete wake-up call. I'd never really had to study in high school—I just showed up, paid attention, and did fine on tests. College was completely different. I failed my first midterm and genuinely thought my life was over and I didn't belong here. But that failure taught me I needed to completely change my approach to studying. By second semester, I'd figured out how to actually study for real, and my grades came up significantly."*
>
> *—First-generation college student*

Socially, focus on finding your people—the ones who will become your support network throughout college. You don't need to be best friends with everyone on your floor or have a huge social circle to post about online. You need a few genuine connections—people who support your success, understand what you're going through, and make you feel less alone in this new environment. Join organizations, study groups, or communities that align with your interests and values.

Practically, learn how the institution actually works. Figure out where the important offices are and what they do. Understand how registration, financial aid, and academic advising work. Build relationships with staff who can help you navigate systems when you run into problems. The practical knowledge you build now will serve you throughout your entire college career and save you enormous stress later.

Emotionally, expect adjustment struggles and don't panic when they inevitably come. Homesickness, loneliness, feeling overwhelmed by everything, questioning whether you belong here—these are completely normal first-year experiences, not signs that something is wrong with you or that you made a mistake coming to college. Reach out for support when you need it, and know that these feelings typically ease as you settle in.

> *"I cried myself to sleep for the first month of college. I missed my family so much it physically hurt, I felt completely out of place among students who seemed so much more prepared, and I was convinced I'd made a terrible mistake coming here. Nobody told me that was normal. I thought I was the only one struggling while everyone else was having the time of their lives. Later I found out almost everyone felt that way at first—they were just hiding it like I was."*
>
> *—First-generation college student*

Research by Tinto and colleagues documented that first-year integration—both academic and social—is the strongest predictor of whether students persist to graduation. Students who feel connected academically (engaged with learning, successful in classes, connected to professors) and socially (connected to peers, involved in campus life, feeling like they belong) are far more likely to stay than those who remain disconnected and isolated.

Watch out for common first-year traps. Partying too much and neglecting academics is an obvious one. But less obvious traps include isolating yourself in your room, not asking for help when you need it, trying to handle everything alone, and not taking advantage of the resources available to support you. The students who struggle most are often those who try to be completely self-sufficient.

First-year priorities to remember: Pass your classes—don't dig yourself into a GPA hole that takes years to climb out of. Build a few meaningful relationships with peers who support your success. Learn how the institution works so you can navigate it effectively. Establish basic habits that support your physical and mental health. Take advantage of support resources before you're in crisis. Don't try to do everything—focus on these fundamentals, and you'll build a solid foundation for everything that follows.

Second Year: Finding Your Direction

The second year is often called the 'sophomore slump' for a reason, and that term captures something real about this stage. The novelty and excitement of college has worn off, but the finish line is still far away and hard to see. You're no longer new enough to get special support designed for first-year students, but you haven't yet committed to a clear path that gives you direction. This year is about exploration, decision-making, and deepening your engagement with college.

Research by Schaller in 2021 described the sophomore year as a time of 'focused exploration'—students are narrowing their options while still actively exploring possibilities. This can feel unsettling because you're supposed to be making important decisions but may not feel ready to commit to anything permanent. That tension is normal and actually productive if you engage with it rather than avoiding it.

Academically, sophomore year often involves choosing or

confirming your major. This decision feels enormous because it seems like it will determine your entire future, and many students feel paralyzed by it. Here's some helpful perspective: your major matters, but it's not a life sentence that locks you into one path forever. Many successful people work in fields completely unrelated to their undergraduate major. What matters more than your specific major is developing transferable skills, building relationships, and discovering what genuinely interests and motivates you.

> *"I changed my major three times during sophomore year alone. First I was pre-med because my family wanted me to be a doctor and that seemed like the path to success. Then I tried business because it seemed practical and safe. Finally I admitted to myself that I actually loved psychology and that's what I wanted to study. That honesty with myself was scary but ultimately liberating. Once I stopped trying to be what others wanted me to be, I found my actual path."*
>
> *—First-generation college student*

Use sophomore year to explore through action, not just through thinking and worrying. Take classes in different areas that interest you. Talk to professors and working professionals about different career paths and what their daily work actually looks like. Try internships, research opportunities, or part-time jobs in fields you're considering. You learn so much more about what fits you by actually doing things than by just thinking about possibly doing them someday.

Socially, sophomore year is often when deeper and more lasting relationships form. The surface-level friendships of freshman year either deepen into something real or gradually fade away, and you discover who your real people are. This is also a good time to build relationships with professors and mentors who can guide your academic and career development in more personalized ways.

The sophomore slump is a real phenomenon, and it catches many students completely off guard because no one warned them about it. You may feel directionless and unmotivated, stuck in a rut where everything feels routine. The excitement and novelty of freshman year is gone, and the clear purpose and momentum of junior and senior year isn't here yet. If you find yourself struggling with motivation or searching for meaning, you're not alone—this is extremely common and it's temporary.

> *"Sophomore year was honestly my hardest year emotionally. Freshman year was exciting because everything was new and I was just trying to survive. But sophomore year just felt like a grind with no clear purpose driving me forward. I wasn't sure why I was doing any of it anymore. I had to really dig deep to reconnect with my reasons for being in college and push through that slump to the other side."*
>
> *—First-generation college student*

Fight the slump by staying connected to your deeper purpose, getting involved in something meaningful that excites you, and remembering that this is a transitional year between stages. You're building toward something even if you can't see it clearly yet from where you're standing now. The decisions and explorations of sophomore year set up the more focused and directed work of your final two years.

Sophomore year priorities: Make real progress on major decisions by exploring actively rather than avoiding them. Explore possibilities through concrete action, not just thought and worry. Deepen relationships with people who genuinely matter to you. Build connections with professors and mentors who can guide you. Stay engaged even when motivation dips. Start thinking seriously about experiences that will build your resume—internships, research, leadership roles.

Third Year: Getting Serious

Junior year is when things get real and serious. You're now in the second half of your college career, and the finish line is visible on the horizon even if it's still some distance away. This year is about commitment—committing to your major field, committing to your direction, and committing to building the experiences that will launch you into whatever comes next after graduation.

Academically, junior year often involves the most challenging coursework in your major. You're past the introductory classes and into the real meat of your field—the advanced content that separates people who are serious about the discipline from those who were just exploring. This is where you discover whether you really love your chosen area or just thought you did from the introductory courses. Either discovery is valuable—one confirms your path and energizes you, the other redirects you before it's too late to change.

This is also when you should be building substantial experiences beyond the classroom that strengthen your profile for whatever comes after graduation. Internships that give you real professional experience, research experiences that deepen your knowledge, leadership positions that develop your skills, substantial projects that demonstrate what you can do—junior year is the time to pursue these seriously and intentionally. Waiting until senior year is often too late because these opportunities take time to develop.

> *"I secured my first real internship the summer after junior year, and it changed absolutely everything about how I saw my education. Suddenly all my coursework made sense because I could see how it applied in the real professional world. That internship also led directly to my*

> *first job offer after graduation. If I'd waited until senior year to start looking for experience, I would have been way behind my peers who started earlier."*
>
> *—First-generation college student*

Start thinking seriously about your post-graduation plans during junior year rather than putting it off. If you're considering graduate school, junior year is when to research programs in depth, prepare for any standardized tests required for admission, and build relationships with professors who can write strong recommendation letters for you. If you're heading directly into the workforce, start understanding what employers in your field are actually looking for and building toward that profile.

Research by Klussman and colleagues in 2021 found that students with strong goal connections—who could clearly see how their current activities connected to their future aspirations—showed greater motivation and achievement than those who felt disconnected from their future. Junior year is an ideal time to strengthen those connections by actively pursuing experiences that bridge your college work and your career plans.

Socially, junior year relationships often become more strategic as well as personal. You're building a professional network whether you fully realize it or not. The professors, supervisors, mentors, and peers you connect with now may be references, collaborators, or career contacts for years or even decades to come. This doesn't mean relationships should become purely transactional—genuine connection still matters most. But recognize that who you know often matters as much as what you know.

> *"I realized during junior year that every relationship was potentially a professional relationship too—not in a fake networking way, but*

in the sense that these connections would last beyond college. My professor became my research advisor, then wrote the grad school recommendations that got me into my program. My internship supervisor became my mentor and eventually offered me my first real job. I started treating relationships more intentionally because of this realization."

—First-generation college student

Junior year can also bring significantly increased stress as the stakes feel higher and the pressure to figure out your entire life intensifies. Take care of yourself through this intensification. Maintain the habits and support systems that keep you healthy physically and mentally. Remember that you don't have to have absolutely everything figured out perfectly—you just need to be making meaningful progress in a direction that makes sense for who you are.

Junior year priorities: Succeed in challenging major coursework that pushes you to grow. Build substantial experiences through internships, research, or leadership. Begin serious planning for post-graduation. Strengthen relationships with professors and mentors who can advocate for you. Maintain your health and wellbeing under increased pressure.

Fourth Year: Finishing Strong and Launching

Senior year is about finishing well and preparing to launch into whatever comes next in your life. It's a year of culmination and transition—celebrating what you've accomplished while preparing for a major life change that can feel both exciting and terrifying. The emotions of senior year are often bittersweet and complicated: excitement about the future mixed with sadness about leaving, anxiety about the unknown mixed with pride in what you've achieved.

Academically, focus on finishing strong all the way to the end. Don't let senioritis—that tempting laziness that comes from feeling like you're almost done—derail you after all you've invested in getting here. Complete your requirements on time, finish any capstone projects or theses with excellence and integrity, and maintain the GPA you've built over years of work. How you finish matters—for graduate school applications, for job references, and for your own sense of integrity and completion.

The job search or graduate school application process dominates much of senior year for many students. This process can be stressful and discouraging, filled with rejection and uncertainty about your worth. Remember that most people don't have everything perfectly figured out by graduation day, and it's completely okay to graduate without a perfect plan lined up. What matters is having direction and momentum, not having every detail resolved.

> *"I applied to probably fifty jobs and got rejected from most of them. It was incredibly discouraging—I started wondering if something was fundamentally wrong with me or if my degree was worthless. Then I finally got one offer, and that's all it took to change everything. I learned that job searching is largely a numbers game, and rejection isn't personal. You only need one yes to start your career."*
>
> *—First-generation college student*

For first-gen students, senior year can bring unique challenges that others don't face. You may be the first in your family to navigate professional job searches or graduate school applications. You may not have networks that lead to easy job connections through family friends or parents' colleagues. You may need to figure out things like professional dress codes, salary negotiation, or relocating for work without family guidance based on experience.

Use every resource available to you during this transition. Career centers exist specifically to help with job searches, resume writing, interview preparation, and career exploration. Professors and mentors can provide advice, perspective, and connections to opportunities. Alumni networks can open doors that would otherwise remain closed. Don't try to figure out the post-graduation transition alone—you have four years of relationship-building to draw on now.

Emotionally, prepare for the complexity of this major life transition. You're leaving a community that has supported you, an identity as a student that has defined you, and routines that have structured your life for years. Even if you're genuinely excited about what's next, grief and anxiety are natural and expected parts of major transitions. Give yourself permission to feel all of it without judgment.

> *"I was surprised by how sad I felt at graduation. I thought I'd just be happy and excited to be done, but I cried more than I expected. I was leaving people I genuinely loved, a place that had become home to me, and a version of myself that had grown so much over four years. Even though I was ready for the next chapter, closing this one was more emotional than I anticipated."*
>
> *—First-generation college student*

Research by Bennett and colleagues in 2022 emphasized that student success extends beyond graduation day—the skills, relationships, and self-knowledge developed in college form a foundation for lifelong success in any field. What you've built in these years doesn't disappear when you walk across the stage to receive your diploma. It goes with you into whatever comes next.

Senior year priorities: Finish academically strong without letting senioritis derail you. Navigate the job search or graduate school application process actively and persistently. Use all available resources and relationships to support your transition. Prepare emotionally for a major life transition. Celebrate what you've accomplished while staying focused on launching well into the next phase of your life.

When Your Path Looks Different

Not everyone follows a straight four-year path through college, and that's completely fine and increasingly common. You might take longer than four years due to work obligations, family responsibilities, financial constraints, or changing academic directions. You might transfer from a community college or another four-year institution. You might take time off for various reasons and return later. You might be an older student with significant life experience. Whatever your particular path, the developmental stages still apply—you just move through them on your own timeline.

If you're taking longer than the traditional four years, don't shame yourself by comparing your timeline to others who seem to be moving faster. What matters is that you're making steady progress and moving toward your goals at a pace that works for your life. Many highly successful people took nonlinear paths to their degrees. The degree you earn after six years is just as valid and valuable as one earned in four—it represents the same achievement and opens the same doors.

> *"I took six years to graduate because I had to work full-time throughout college and could only take classes part-time. Sometimes I felt embarrassed when people asked why I was still in school while my high school friends had already graduated and started careers. But I finished. I earned my degree while supporting myself financially and helping my family. That's not something to be ashamed of—that's something to be deeply*

proud of."

—First-generation college student

If you're a transfer student, you face unique challenges of starting over socially while being academically advanced. You may feel caught between worlds—not a freshman experiencing everything for the first time but not established at your new school either. Be intentional about building relationships and learning your new institution quickly. The integration that others had years to build, you need to build faster and more deliberately.

If you're an older or returning student, you bring valuable life experience but may sometimes feel out of place among younger classmates who seem to be at a different life stage. Your maturity and perspective are genuine assets, even if they sometimes make you feel different from those around you. Seek out other non-traditional students and create community with people whose paths look like yours.

Research by Toutkoushian and colleagues in 2021 noted that first-gen students are more likely than continuing-generation students to follow non-traditional paths to their degrees. This is often a reflection of the real constraints many first-gen students face in their lives, not a reflection of ability or commitment. Honor your path, whatever it looks like.

Wherever you are in your journey, the key is to be intentional about the stage you're in rather than wishing you were somewhere else. What are the developmental tasks of this particular stage? What should you be focusing on right now? What opportunities should you be pursuing? What challenges should you be preparing for? Answer these questions for your specific situation, not based on what year you're technically classified as according to credit hours.

What Research Helps Us Understand

Research shows that college persistence and success follow developmental patterns, with each year bringing distinct challenges and opportunities. First-year integration predicts long-term success more than almost any other factor. Sophomore year exploration and decision-making lay crucial groundwork for commitment. Junior year intensification builds the experiences that prepare students for post-graduation success. Senior year transition requires both closure and launching. Students who understand and prepare for each stage navigate their journeys more successfully than those who are surprised by stage-specific challenges. Non-traditional paths are increasingly common, especially among first-gen students, and lead to equally valid degrees and outcomes.

The Huddle

Take time to reflect on these questions thoughtfully, alone or with others.

Take time alone or with others to work through these questions. They help you understand where you are in your journey and prepare for what's ahead.

Begin by considering this: what are the main priorities and challenges of each college year described in this chapter? List the key focus areas for freshman, sophomore, junior, and senior years.

Next, reflect on this: explain why the first year is considered the highest-risk period for dropping out. What factors contribute to this, and how can students reduce their risk?

Take a moment to think about this: based on where you are in your college journey right now, what are the two or three most important things you should be focusing on this semester?

Consider this honestly: think about your own path through college so far. How has it followed or differed from the typical pattern? What stage-specific challenges have you faced?

Now ask yourself: assess how well you're addressing the priorities of your current stage. What are you doing well? What needs more attention?

Reflect carefully on this: create a roadmap for your remaining time in college. What do you need to accomplish or experience each semester to be ready for whatever comes after graduation? Your path through college is uniquely yours, shaped by your background, your circumstances, and the choices you make along the way. No two students walk exactly the same road, and the milestones that matter most are the ones that align with your own values and aspirations rather than someone else's expectations.

Finally, consider this: write advice for a student one year behind you in their journey. What do you wish you had known at the stage they're currently in? What would have made that year easier or more successful?

Every stage of your journey matters. Where you are right now is exactly where you need to be—focus there, and the future will take care of itself. Remember that these year-by-year milestones are guidelines, not rigid requirements. Your path through college may not follow a straight line, and that is perfectly normal. Students who transfer, take time off, change majors, or move at a different pace are not behind. They are simply navigating a journey that looks different from the traditional four-year template. What matters is not whether you match someone else's timeline but whether you are making intentional choices that align with your values, your circumstances, and your goals.

The students who thrive in college are not the ones who never deviate from the plan. They are the ones who learn to adapt their plan as they grow and change. Each year of college presents unique challenges and unique opportunities. By understanding what to expect and preparing yourself accordingly, you position yourself not just to survive each phase but to extract the maximum growth and benefit from it. Your college experience is yours to shape, and every year you invest in your own development brings you closer to the person you are becoming.

CHAPTER 10

AI as Your Learning Partner

AI as Your Personal Tutor: Using Technology to Learn Smarter

> *"I didn't have money for a private tutor, and I felt embarrassed going to the tutoring center because I thought everyone would see how much I was struggling. Then I discovered I could ask AI to explain things to me at 2am when nobody was watching. It was like having a patient teacher available whenever I needed one, who never made me feel stupid for asking basic questions."*
>
> *—First-generation college student*

Something remarkable has happened in the past few years that fundamentally changes what's possible for students like you. Artificial intelligence tools—programs like ChatGPT, Claude, and others—have become widely available and can serve as personal tutors accessible around the clock, at no cost, with infinite patience and zero judgment. For first-generation students who may not have access to expensive private tutoring or family members who can help with challenging coursework, this technology represents an extraordinary opportunity to level the playing field in ways that weren't possible even a few years ago.

The student who opens this chapter discovered what many first-gen students are now finding: AI can be a judgment-free learning partner available whenever you need help. No waiting for office hours when you're stuck at midnight. No feeling embarrassed in front of peers at the tutoring center. No cost that strains an already tight budget. Just patient explanation, as many times as you need it, in whatever way helps you personally understand best.

But AI tools are just that—tools. Like any tool, they can be used well or poorly. They can accelerate your learning dramatically or undermine it completely. They can help you develop deeper understanding or enable you to avoid the productive struggle that produces real growth. This chapter will teach you how to use AI as an effective learning partner while avoiding the pitfalls that could hurt your education and your academic integrity.

This isn't a chapter about cheating or taking shortcuts—far from it. It's about using available technology strategically to support genuine learning, the same way you might use a calculator in math class or a spell-checker when writing. The goal is to learn more effectively, not to avoid learning altogether. Used wisely and ethically, AI can be one of the most powerful educational resources you have access to during your college years.

For first-gen students especially, learning to use AI effectively is a skill that will serve you throughout college and well into your career. This technology isn't going away—it's becoming more central to how work gets done across virtually every field and profession. Understanding how to leverage it for learning now prepares you for a future where AI literacy is as essential as computer literacy became for previous generations.

What AI Can Do for Your Learning

Let's start with the fundamentals of what AI tutoring tools can actually do for you as a learner. Understanding these capabilities helps you know when and how to use them most effectively in your studies. AI can explain concepts in multiple ways until you finally understand them. If the textbook explanation doesn't make sense to you, you can ask AI to explain the same concept differently—using analogies to things you already know, simpler everyday language, real-world examples from your own experience, or step-by-step breakdowns that take complex ideas apart. You can keep asking for different explanations until something finally clicks and makes sense. A human tutor might understandably get frustrated after explaining something three or four times; AI never does and never will.

> *"I was completely lost in my statistics class—it felt like the professor was speaking a foreign language. The professor explained standard deviation one way, the textbook explained it another way, and neither made any sense to me no matter how many times I read it. I asked the AI to explain it like I was in middle school, then asked for a real-world example using something I actually cared about—basketball stats. Suddenly it clicked for the first time. I could ask for exactly the explanation I personally needed."*
>
> *—First-generation college student*

AI can help you practice and test yourself as much as you need. You can ask it to generate practice problems similar to what you'll see on your upcoming exams. You can ask it to quiz you on material you're studying for any class. You can work through problems step by step and get feedback on exactly where you went wrong and why. This kind of active practice with immediate feedback is exactly what decades of research shows produces real, lasting learning—and AI makes it available on demand whenever you need it.

AI can help you understand your assignments and get started when you're feeling stuck and paralyzed. When you're staring at a blank page not knowing how to begin a paper, AI can help you brainstorm ideas, create an initial outline, or understand what the assignment is actually asking for. It can't write your paper for you—and you absolutely shouldn't let it—but it can help you overcome the paralysis of not knowing where to start, which is often the hardest part.

AI can serve as a writing coach, giving you detailed feedback on drafts before you submit them for a grade. You can ask it to identify weaknesses in your argument, suggest specific ways to improve clarity and flow, point out grammatical issues and awkward phrasing, or check whether you've actually addressed all parts of the prompt. This is similar to what the writing center does, but available at 2am when the writing center is closed and you're desperately working to meet a deadline.

AI can help you prepare for class by previewing material before lectures so you're not hearing everything for the first time. You can ask it to summarize the key concepts in a chapter you're about to read, explain unfamiliar terms you'll encounter, or give you background context that will help the lecture make more sense when you hear it. Coming to class already somewhat familiar with the basics helps you engage at a higher level during the lecture itself.

Research by Mollick and Mollick in 2023 found that students who used AI tools strategically as learning aids showed significantly improved understanding and performance, while those who used AI to avoid learning showed worse outcomes than students who didn't use AI at all. The difference was entirely in how the tool was used—as a learning accelerator versus a learning replacement.

Using AI as a Learning Partner, Not a Crutch

The key to using AI effectively is treating it as a learning partner that helps you understand and grow—not as a shortcut that does your thinking for you. This distinction makes all the difference between AI that genuinely accelerates your education and AI that fundamentally undermines it. Use AI to understand concepts deeply, not to produce work you submit. When you're struggling with a concept, use AI to get explanations until you truly understand the material. But then close the AI and work on problems yourself using only what's in your head. Test whether you actually learned by doing the work independently without any assistance. If you can't do it without the AI helping you step by step, you haven't actually learned it yet—you've just borrowed understanding temporarily.

Ask AI to teach you how to do something, not to do it for you. Instead of asking 'What's the answer to this problem?' ask 'How do I approach this type of problem in general?' Instead of asking AI to write your introduction paragraph, ask 'What makes a strong introduction for this type of essay, and what should I include?' The goal is always to build your own capability that you can use independently, not to outsource your thinking to a machine.

> *"My personal rule is simple: AI can explain anything to me as many times as I need, but I have to do the actual graded work myself. When I'm stuck on a math problem, I'll ask AI to explain the underlying concept or show me how to approach similar problems step by step. But then I close the chat completely and work through my actual homework problems on my own paper. If I can't do it without AI watching over my shoulder, I know I need to study more, not just copy more."*
>
> *—First-generation college student*

Use AI to fill gaps in your foundational understanding, especially gaps from before college. First-gen students sometimes arrive at college with gaps in preparation that make advanced material harder to grasp—not because of any lack of ability, but simply because their high schools may not have offered the same preparation. AI can help you quickly fill those gaps without embarrassment or judgment. If you're in calculus but feeling shaky on algebra fundamentals, AI can give you a rapid review. If you're writing a research paper but never properly learned citation format, AI can teach you step by step.

Use AI to get unstuck when you hit a wall, then continue independently with your own thinking. When you reach a point where you don't know how to proceed and feel completely stuck, AI can give you just enough help to get moving again. Ask for a hint rather than a full solution. Ask what concept you should review rather than asking for the answer directly. Use AI to overcome stuck points and barriers, then do all the remaining work yourself.

Review AI's responses critically rather than accepting them blindly and uncritically. AI can make mistakes, present outdated information, or give explanations that are technically correct but actually misleading in important ways. Always verify important information through other reliable sources like your textbook or professor. Treat AI as a helpful but imperfect study partner whose suggestions you thoughtfully evaluate rather than automatically trust without question.

Research by Chen and colleagues in 2023 emphasized that the learning benefits of AI depend entirely on maintaining cognitive engagement—actively thinking, questioning, processing, and struggling—rather than passively receiving information without effort. AI works best when it prompts and supports your thinking, not when it replaces your thinking entirely.

Practical Strategies for Different Subjects

Different subjects call for different ways of using AI as a learning tool. Here are specific strategies that work well for the common types of courses you'll encounter in college.

For math and quantitative subjects, use AI to understand concepts and methods deeply, then practice extensively on your own without any assistance. Ask AI to explain why a formula works, not just how to mechanically use it. Ask it to walk through the underlying logic of proofs. Ask for multiple practice problems and work through them yourself before checking your answers. If you get something wrong, ask AI to explain specifically where your reasoning went wrong and why—this targeted feedback on your mistakes accelerates learning dramatically.

> *"In calculus, I use AI as my concept explainer and nothing more. When we learn a new technique, I have AI explain the underlying idea until it actually makes intuitive sense to me—not just the mechanical steps, but why those particular steps work mathematically. Then I do tons of practice problems completely on my own with the AI closed. I'll only go back to AI if I'm absolutely stuck, and even then I ask for a hint about what concept to review, not the answer itself."*
>
> *—First-generation college student*

For writing-intensive subjects, use AI as a brainstorming partner and editor, but do all your own actual writing. Ask AI to help you generate ideas to write about, identify holes or weaknesses in your argument, or improve clarity in specific passages that feel awkward. Share your drafts and ask for constructive feedback, just as you would with the writing center or a peer reviewer. But every word you submit must be yours, written by you, expressing your own genuine thoughts and analysis.

For science courses, use AI to understand mechanisms and connections between concepts. Science is full of complex processes with many interconnected steps—AI can break these down and explain how all the pieces fit together into a coherent whole. Ask it to explain what happens at the molecular level, or why a chemical reaction proceeds the way it does, or how one biological system connects to another. This deep conceptual understanding helps you apply knowledge to new situations you haven't seen before.

For humanities and social sciences, use AI to explore multiple perspectives and deepen your own analysis. Ask AI to present different scholarly interpretations of a text or historical event. Ask it to explain theoretical frameworks you can apply in your own analysis. Use it to identify gaps in your argument or counterarguments you should address to strengthen your paper. But your interpretations, arguments, and conclusions must be genuinely yours—AI helps you think more deeply, not think for you.

For language learning, AI is an incredibly patient conversation partner available around the clock. Practice writing sentences in your target language and get immediate feedback on grammar and word choice. Have conversations in your target language at whatever level you're currently at. Ask for detailed explanations of grammar rules with multiple examples until they make sense. Request vocabulary in meaningful context rather than just isolated word lists. The unlimited, patient practice opportunity is genuinely invaluable for language acquisition.

For test preparation across all subjects, have AI generate practice questions similar to what you'll actually face on upcoming exams. Work through them yourself without any help, then use AI to understand any concepts you missed or got wrong. Ask AI to identify the most important topics likely to be tested based on the material you've covered in class. Use it to fill gaps in your understanding before the exam, never during it.

Maintaining Your Academic Integrity

Let's be completely direct about something important: using AI to cheat is still cheating, and the consequences can be severe —including failing courses, academic probation, or even expulsion from your institution. More importantly, cheating with AI defeats the entire purpose of your education. You're here to learn and grow as a person and professional, not to collect credentials without the knowledge and skills they're supposed to represent.

The line between helpful use and academic dishonesty can sometimes feel blurry, but a clear principle guides the distinction: are you using AI to enhance your own learning and thinking, or to substitute for it entirely? Using AI to understand a concept better is legitimate and encouraged. Having AI write your essay for you is not. Using AI to get feedback on your own draft is legitimate. Submitting AI-generated text as your own work is not and never will be.

Know your specific institution's and professors' policies on AI use. These policies vary significantly from school to school and even from class to class. Some professors actively welcome AI as a learning tool with appropriate disclosure of how you used it. Others prohibit any AI use whatsoever on their assignments. When in doubt about what's permitted, ask directly —professors appreciate students who proactively seek clarity. Following the specific rules in each class protects you from unintentional violations that could have serious lasting consequences.

> *"I made a mistake early on in my first semester —I used AI too much on a paper and the professor immediately noticed the writing wasn't in my usual voice. I was completely honest about what I'd done when confronted, and while I had to redo the entire assignment from scratch, I didn't face serious academic consequences because it was clearly a misunderstanding about appropriate use rather than intentional cheating. That experience taught me to always ask professors about their specific AI policies upfront before I even start an assignment."*
>
> *—First-generation college student*

When AI helps you with an assignment, disclose it appropriately if your professor's policy requires or permits disclosure. Many professors actually appreciate transparency about how you used AI in your learning process. A simple note explaining that you used AI to help understand concepts, brainstorm initial ideas, or get feedback on drafts demonstrates integrity while showing you engaged in genuine learning with the AI as a support tool.

Remember that AI-generated work often has detectable patterns and can include subtle errors, generic content, or a writing voice that doesn't match your established style. Professors are becoming increasingly skilled at recognizing AI-produced text, and detection tools are improving rapidly. But more fundamentally, if you're having AI do your work for you, you're stealing from yourself—paying tuition for an education while actively avoiding the learning that makes that education valuable.

The test that matters most is this: after using AI, do you understand the material well enough to explain it in your own words, apply it to new situations, and build on it without any AI assistance? If yes, you've used AI appropriately as a learning tool. If no, you've used it as a crutch that's actually preventing your real learning and growth.

Understanding AI's Limitations

AI is a genuinely powerful tool, but it has real limitations you need to understand to use it wisely and effectively. Overrelying on AI or trusting it blindly without verification can lead you seriously astray.

AI can be confidently wrong about things. AI tools generate responses that sound authoritative and certain even when they're partially or completely incorrect. They can invent plausible-sounding facts, cite sources that don't actually exist, or give explanations that sound reasonable but are fundamentally mistaken in important ways. Always verify important information through textbooks, peer-reviewed sources, or your professors—especially for high-stakes assignments where accuracy matters.

AI doesn't know what you specifically need to learn for your particular classes. Your professor designed your course with specific learning goals and approaches in mind. AI doesn't know what your class has actually covered, what your professor emphasizes as most important, or what will be on your exams. Use AI to supplement your course materials, not to replace them entirely. Your textbook and professor's explanations should always remain your primary sources for what matters in your specific courses.

> *"I learned the hard way that AI doesn't always match what my specific professor teaches. I studied a concept extensively using AI explanations, and on the exam I answered based on what AI taught me—but it was different from how my professor explained and approached that same concept, and I lost significant points. Now I always cross-reference AI explanations with my actual class notes and assigned textbook."*
>
> *—First-generation college student*

AI can't replace human connection in your education. Learning from professors and peers involves far more than just absorbing information. It includes building relationships that support your success over time, developing professional networks for your career, and learning to communicate effectively with real people about complex ideas. AI is a supplement to human learning environments, never a substitute for them.

AI doesn't know your personal context, circumstances, or goals. A human tutor, advisor, or mentor can understand your specific situation, your learning style, your long-term goals, and your current challenges in ways AI simply cannot. For advice that requires understanding your whole situation—academic planning, career decisions, personal challenges affecting your studies—human guidance is essential and irreplaceable.

AI knowledge has cutoff dates and gaps. AI tools are trained on data up to certain dates and may not have information about current events, recent discoveries, or the latest developments in rapidly changing fields. They may also have significant gaps in specialized or technical areas. For cutting-edge research, current events, or specialized professional knowledge, other sources are essential.

Research by Kasneci and colleagues in 2023 identified both the genuine promise and the real limitations of AI in educational settings, emphasizing that the most effective approach combines AI tools with traditional learning resources and human instruction rather than relying on AI alone as a primary learning source.

Combining AI with Human Support

The most effective approach uses AI as one tool among many in your learning toolkit—complementing rather than replacing human support from professors, tutors, advisors, and peers. Each type of resource offers something valuable that the others cannot provide.

Use AI for immediate help and unlimited practice opportunities. When you're studying late at night and stuck on a concept, AI is there and available. When you need twenty practice problems, but the textbook only has five, AI can generate more on demand. When you want to review a concept without embarrassment or judgment, AI provides a safe space. These are AI's unique strengths that no other resource can match.

Use professors for course-specific expertise and validation of your understanding. Your professor knows exactly what you need to learn for their class and how it fits into broader disciplinary knowledge. Office hours with professors also build relationships that can lead to research opportunities, strong recommendation letters, and ongoing mentorship throughout your career. AI can't provide any of this—only human relationships can.

Use tutoring centers and peer tutors for collaborative learning experiences. Working through problems with another person—especially someone who recently learned the material themselves—offers a different kind of learning than solo study with AI. Human tutors can notice where you're confused even when you don't realize it yourself, and they can share strategies that worked for them personally when they were learning the same material.

> *"I use AI when I'm first trying to understand something new and when I'm practicing on my own late at night. But I go to office hours when I need to make sure I'm on the right track for what my specific professor actually wants and expects. And I study with classmates when I need the motivation and accountability of learning with other people who are struggling with the same material. Each resource fills a different need in my learning."*
>
> *—First-generation college student*

Use advisors for guidance that requires knowing your unique situation. Academic advisors, career counselors, and mentors can help you navigate decisions that depend on your specific circumstances, goals, and constraints. AI can provide general information about options and possibilities, but humans who actually know you can provide personalized guidance tailored to your situation.

Use peers for accountability and community. Study groups, peer support, and shared struggle are important parts of the college experience that AI simply can't replicate. The motivation that comes from learning alongside others, the relationships you build through shared challenges—these matter for your success and your wellbeing in ways that go beyond just academic learning.

Think of AI as extending your access to learning support, not replacing the human relationships that matter most. First-gen students sometimes have less access to knowledgeable human help than peers whose families include college graduates who can advise them. AI can partially close that gap and provide some of what you might be missing. But it works best when combined with the human support you're building through the relationships we discussed in earlier chapters.

Getting Started with AI Tutoring

If you haven't already started using AI as a learning tool, here's how to begin in a way that sets you up for effective, ethical use from the start.

Choose your tools wisely. Several AI tools are available for free or at low cost. ChatGPT, Claude, and Google's Gemini are among the most capable general-purpose options. Try a few different ones and see which interface and style of response works best for you personally. Different tools have different strengths—some are better at math explanations, others at writing feedback, others at general explanation.

Learn to prompt effectively for better results. The quality of AI responses depends heavily on how you ask your questions. Be specific about what you need and where you're stuck. Provide context about what you already understand and what's confusing you. Ask follow-up questions when the first response doesn't fully help. Tell AI if you need a simpler explanation or a different approach—it will adjust.

> *"I got way better, more useful results once I learned to give AI proper context about my situation. Instead of just asking 'explain photosynthesis,' I now say something like 'I'm in introductory biology, I understand that plants need sunlight, but I'm confused about exactly how light energy becomes chemical energy in the chloroplast. Can you explain just that specific step in simple terms with an analogy?' The more specific I am about what I need, the more helpful the response becomes."*

—First-generation college student

Start with low-stakes practice before using AI on important assignments. Before relying on AI for significant graded work, practice using it for general studying and concept review where the stakes are lower. This helps you learn what it does well and poorly, how to prompt effectively, and how to integrate it into your learning process before you depend on it for anything important.

Develop your personal guidelines for AI use. Decide in advance how you'll use AI and where you'll draw firm lines. What will you use AI for without hesitation? What lines won't you cross under any circumstances? How will you make sure you're actually learning, not just getting answers? Having clear personal rules helps you use AI consistently and ethically across all your courses.

Regularly test your independent ability without any AI assistance. Periodically close the AI and test whether you can do the work without it. If you're using AI to learn math, can you solve problems without AI help? If you're using AI for writing feedback, can you identify weaknesses in your own writing yourself? Your ability to perform without AI is the real measure of your learning.

Stay informed as technology evolves rapidly. AI tools are improving quickly, and norms around their use are still developing across institutions. Pay attention to your institution's evolving policies, new tools that become available, and emerging best practices for educational use. Being an informed, adaptable user will serve you throughout your education and career.

What Research Helps Us Understand

Research on AI in education is rapidly evolving, but early findings suggest that AI tools can significantly enhance learning when used as cognitive aids that prompt thinking and explanation rather than as substitutes for student effort. Studies show improved outcomes when students use AI to understand concepts, generate practice opportunities, and receive feedback—but worse outcomes when students use AI to avoid cognitive struggle. The key variable is whether AI use maintains or undermines active learning and engagement. Effective use requires understanding AI's limitations, verifying information through other sources, and maintaining human connections and institutional engagement that predict college success.

The Huddle

Take time to reflect on these questions thoughtfully, alone or with others.

Take time alone or with others to work through these questions. They help you develop a thoughtful, effective approach to using AI in your learning.

Begin by considering this: list three appropriate ways to use AI as a learning tool and three inappropriate ways that would constitute academic dishonesty. What's the key principle that distinguishes them?

Next, reflect on this: explain in your own words why using AI to understand a concept is different from using AI to produce your work. Why does this distinction matter for your actual learning?

Take a moment to think about this: identify a subject or concept you're currently struggling with in one of your classes. Write out specific prompts you could use to get helpful explanations from AI while maintaining your own learning engagement.

Consider this honestly: analyze your current use of AI (if any). Are you using it in ways that build your understanding and capability? Are there ways you've been tempted to use it that might undermine your learning?

Now ask yourself: evaluate the AI policies in your current courses. Do your professors allow, encourage, restrict, or prohibit AI use? How will you adjust your approach appropriately for different classes?

Reflect carefully on this: create your personal AI use guidelines—specific rules you'll follow to ensure AI enhances your learning rather than replacing it. What will you use AI for? What lines won't you cross?

Finally, consider this: design a study session that strategically combines AI tools with other learning resources (textbook, notes, practice problems, study partners). How will each resource contribute to your learning?

AI is a tool—what matters is how you use it. Used wisely, it's like having a patient tutor available whenever you need one. Use that power to learn more, not to learn less.

CHAPTER 11

Putting It All Together: Your Action Plan

Pulling It All Together: Your Action Plan for Success

> *"Reading about success is one thing. Actually, doing it is something else entirely. What changed everything for me was when I stopped just absorbing information and started putting it into practice—one small step at a time, one day at a time. Knowledge only matters when you actually use it to change your life."*
>
> *—First-generation college student*

You've made it through ten chapters full of research, strategies, stories, and reflection questions. You've learned about identity development and how college transforms you in ways you might not have expected. You've discovered study strategies that actually work according to decades of cognitive science research. You've explored habit formation that sustains you when motivation inevitably fades. You've considered how to build relationships that create support networks strong enough to carry you through difficulty. You've examined resilience and what it really takes to bounce back from setbacks.

That's a tremendous amount of information to absorb and remember. But here's the truth that separates people who change from people who just read about change: information alone doesn't change anything in your actual life. You can read every book about college success ever written. You can attend every workshop and seminar. You can know all the right strategies and quote all the research.

The student who opens this final chapter names the crucial truth that makes all the difference: knowledge only matters when you use it. She didn't transform her college experience by learning about good strategies—she transformed it by actually implementing those strategies, one small step at a time, building momentum through consistent action. That's what this chapter will help you do.

This chapter serves as both a comprehensive summary of everything we've covered throughout the book and a practical action planning guide for putting it all into practice immediately. We'll revisit the core ideas from each chapter to refresh your memory and ensure the key principles are clear. But more importantly, we'll focus on concrete steps you can take starting today—not someday, not next semester, but today. By the end of this chapter, you'll have a personalized action plan tailored specifically to where you are right now in your unique journey.

One crucial warning before we begin: don't try to do everything at once. That's a recipe for overwhelming yourself and almost certainly failing at everything. Instead, focus on a few key areas that matter most for your current situation and circumstances. Small, consistent actions add up to dramatic changes over time. The goal isn't perfection—it's steady progress in the direction you want to go, one manageable step at a time.

This chapter is designed to be practical and actionable above all else. Read it with a pen in hand or a notes app open on your phone ready to capture your thoughts. Mark the ideas that resonate most strongly with your current situation. Write down specific commitments you're genuinely willing to make and follow through on. Then actually follow through on those commitments, starting today—not tomorrow, not next week, not when things calm down, but today.

The Core Ideas Worth Remembering

The chapters in this book have given you a comprehensive foundation for college success. You explored the seven dimensions of personal growth that college activates, from building competence and managing emotions to developing your identity and clarifying your purpose. You learned that the hidden curriculum of college learning requires different strategies than high school, and that effective studying demands active retrieval, spaced practice, and metacognitive awareness rather than passive rereading.

You discovered that habits, not motivation, carry you through the long stretches of college life, and that small consistent actions built on identity produce more lasting change than willpower alone. You learned that relationships are not just social comforts but structural support for persistence, and that resilience is not about being unbreakable but about knowing how to recover, adapt, and continue with awareness.

You explored how to plan with purpose rather than just react to deadlines, how to prepare for life beyond graduation while still in school, how to navigate challenges year by year as your college journey evolves, and how to use AI as a genuine learning partner without undermining your own growth. Each of these themes connects to a single insight at the heart of this book: success in college is not about being perfect or never struggling. It is about building systems, seeking support, and staying engaged with your own development even when the path is unclear.

Assessing Where You Are Right Now

Before you can make an effective action plan that will actually work for you, you need to honestly assess where you currently stand in your college journey. Not where you wish you were or where you think you should be, or where others expect you to be—where you actually are right now, with all your genuine strengths and all your real areas for growth. This assessment isn't about harsh judgment or making yourself feel bad about shortcomings. It's about gaining the clarity that enables effective, targeted action.

Consider each major area we've covered throughout this

book and rate yourself honestly, without either excessive self-criticism or comfortable self-deception. In your academic habits and study practices, are you consistently using effective strategies that research shows actually work, or are you just doing what feels comfortable and hoping for the best? In your relationships and support network, do you have the connections you genuinely need to sustain you through difficulty, or are you more isolated than you'd like to admit?

> "I had to get really honest with myself about where I actually was in my college journey, not where I wanted to pretend I was or where I thought I should be. I realized through honest reflection that my study habits were actually terrible even though I kept telling myself they were fine because I'd always gotten by before.
>
> *—First-generation college student*

Research by Collings and Eaton in 2021 found that students who accurately assessed their own situations and adjusted their approaches accordingly showed significantly better outcomes than those who either overestimated or underestimated where they actually stood. Self-awareness is a foundational requirement for effective action. You simply cannot fix problems you won't acknowledge exist, and you can't build on strengths you don't recognize you have.

Think specifically about your current challenges and obstacles. What's getting in the way of your success right now, today, this semester? Is it academic struggles in specific classes or subjects? Is it time management problems and feeling constantly behind? Is it financial stress affecting your ability to focus on academics? Is it relationship issues or painful isolation from meaningful connection? Is it mental health challenges that you've been ignoring or minimizing?

Also think carefully about your current strengths—and everyone has genuine strengths, even if they're hard to see when you're struggling or feeling down about yourself. What's already working reasonably well in your life right now? Where are you experiencing at least some success, even if that success feels partial or inconsistent? What resources do you already have access to that you could leverage more effectively if you were intentional about it? What skills have you already developed that you can build upon? Building on existing strengths is often easier and more sustainable than only focusing on weaknesses, problems, and deficiencies.

Be as specific as humanly possible in your self-assessment. 'I'm not doing well' is far too vague to act on in any meaningful way. 'I'm failing chemistry because I don't study consistently and I'm afraid to go to office hours because I don't want to look stupid in front of the professor' is specific enough to address with concrete actions. The more precise and detailed your understanding of where you currently are, the more targeted and effective your action plan can be.

Choosing Your Focus Areas

You absolutely cannot work on everything at once, not being ambitious, it's setting yourself up for certain failure through overwhelming paralysis. Trying to improve in every area simultaneously leads to spreading yourself so thin that you usually end up making real progress in none of them. Instead, choose just two or three priority areas to focus on with real intensity and commitment right now. You can address other important areas later once you've made progress—this is about identifying what needs your attention most urgently given where you currently are.

How do you choose which priorities deserve your focused attention? Consider several important factors to make this decision wisely and strategically. What's causing the most pain or creating the biggest problems in your life right now on a daily basis? What would have the biggest positive ripple effect if you improved it, potentially improving other areas as well? What's most connected to your current stage of the college journey and its particular demands? What feels most actionable and achievable given your current energy, available time, and accessible resources?

Some common priority patterns emerge for different challenging situations that students frequently face. If you're struggling academically and your grades are suffering or you're at risk of academic probation, focus primarily on study strategies and actively using academic support resources like tutoring and office hours. If you're feeling isolated, lonely, and disconnected with no real meaningful connections on campus, focus primarily on deliberate relationship building.

> *"I desperately wanted to fix absolutely everything at once—my struggling grades, my nonexistent social life, my constant stress levels, my precarious financial situation, my deteriorating health, my complicated relationship with my family, everything that felt broken or inadequate. My academic advisor helped me see that trying to fix everything simultaneously was not only unrealistic but actually counterproductive and likely to result in fixing nothing. She asked me one powerful clarifying question: 'What one thing, if it improved significantly, would make everything else in your life easier to handle?' That single question helped me focus on what genuinely mattered most right now."*
>
> *—First-generation college student*

Carefully consider the ripple effects and interconnections between different priority areas. Some changes create positive cascades that improve multiple areas at once with a single focused effort. For example, building one strong study group addresses both academics and relationships simultaneously through the same activity. Establishing better sleep habits improves both physical health and academic performance together. Finding meaningful involvement in a campus organization addresses both purpose and relationships at the same time. Look strategically for these high-leverage changes that multiply benefits across multiple areas of your life.

Research by Klussman and colleagues in 2021 found that focused, committed goal pursuit produced significantly better measurable results than scattered efforts spread across many different goals. Students who committed deeply and consistently to a few important priorities outperformed those who spread their attention thin across many areas trying to improve everything at once. Depth consistently beats breadth when it comes to making real, lasting change in your life and habits.

Write down your two or three priority areas right now before continuing to the next section. Be as specific as possible about exactly what you want to improve in each area. These priorities will guide everything else in your action plan and determine where you invest your limited time and energy.

Building Your Specific Action Plan

Now it's time to get truly specific about what you'll actually do differently starting immediately. For each priority area you've identified, you need concrete, specific actions—not vague intentions to 'do better' but actual steps you can take starting this week. Vague intentions and general plans to improve don't create real change in behavior. Specific, detailed plans with clear actions, times, and places do.

For each of your identified priorities, answer all of these questions thoroughly and specifically: What specific actions will you take? When exactly will you do them—what day of the week and what specific time? Where will you do them? How will you remember and actually follow through when the scheduled time arrives? What obstacles might realistically get in the way of following through? How will you handle those obstacles when they inevitably arise? Who can support you in this effort and help hold you accountable? How will you know if you're actually making progress over time?

Make your planned actions as specific and initially small as possible—smaller than you think is necessary. 'Study more' is far too vague to actually execute consistently. 'Use active recall techniques for chemistry every Tuesday and Thursday from 2-3pm in the library's quiet study room on the third floor' is specific enough to actually do without having to make decisions or exert willpower in the moment.

> *"The absolute game changer for me was making my plans ridiculously, almost embarrassingly specific—way more specific and detailed than I initially thought was necessary or reasonable. Not just 'go to office hours sometime when I have a chance' but 'go to Professor Johnson's office hours every single Wednesday at exactly 10am with at least one specific question written down on paper before I walk in the door.' Not just 'exercise more often' but 'walk to the campus recreation center Monday, Wednesday, and Friday right after my 9am class ends, before I go anywhere else or check my phone.' That level of specificity made things actually happen instead of remaining good intentions."*
>
> *—First-generation college student*

Build accountability into your plan from the very start. Research consistently shows that people are significantly more likely to follow through on commitments when there's some meaningful form of accountability beyond just their own willpower and good intentions. Tell someone you trust about your plan and explicitly ask them to check in with you about it regularly. Find an accountability partner who has similar goals and commit to supporting each other. Track your progress somewhere visible where you'll see it daily. Create meaningful consequences—positive or negative—for following through or not following through.

Anticipate obstacles realistically and plan how you'll handle them in advance before they actually happen. What will you do when you don't feel like following through because you're tired, stressed, or just not in the mood? What will you do when something unexpected interferes with your carefully made plan? What will you do when you fail to follow through one day despite your best intentions and sincere commitment? Having these contingency responses planned out in advance makes it dramatically easier to stay on track when challenges inevitably arise, because you're not trying to problem-solve in the difficult moment itself.

Start with implementation intentions—if-then plans that automatically link specific situations to specific actions without requiring willpower or decision-making in the moment. For example: 'If I finish my morning class, then I will go directly to the library to study for one hour without stopping anywhere else first.' 'If I notice I'm feeling isolated and lonely, then I will text a friend to meet for coffee within 24 hours.' 'If I get a grade below 80% on any assignment or exam, then I will visit the professor's office hours within two days to discuss what went wrong.' These automatic triggers make following through much easier because you've already made the decision in advance.

Creating Systems That Support You

Individual actions matter, but systems matter significantly more for long-term sustained success that lasts beyond initial motivation. A system is a structure in your life that makes good behavior more automatic and requires less willpower, while making bad behavior more difficult and inconvenient. Instead of relying on willpower and motivation—which are finite resources that deplete throughout the day and fluctuate unpredictably—you deliberately design your environment, routines, and social context to support the outcomes you want.

Think carefully and critically about your physical environment and how it shapes your behavior. Where do you typically try to study? Is that location actually set up to support focus and deep concentration, or does it invite distraction and procrastination through easy access to entertainment, social media, or other people? Where do you spend most of your waking time on a typical day? Do those places support your goals and the person you want to become, or do they undermine your intentions? What objects and devices are easily accessible to you throughout the day?

Think carefully about your time structure and how you manage the hours in your day and week. Do you have regular, protected times blocked out for important activities like studying, exercise, and connecting with friends, or do you just hope to somehow fit them in whenever you happen to have free time?

> "I completely restructured my entire week around my stated priorities after realizing my old approach wasn't working. Sunday evening I plan the entire week ahead in detail. Monday, Wednesday, and Friday I study in the library from 6-9pm—that time is completely non-negotiable with no exceptions allowed except genuine emergencies. Tuesday and Thursday evenings are designated for my student organization involvement and intentional social time with friends.
>
> —*First-generation college student*

Think carefully about your social environment and the

people who surround you regularly. Who do you spend significant time with on a daily and weekly basis? Do those people genuinely support your goals and encourage your growth, or do they pull you away from your priorities through their own habits, attitudes, and lifestyle choices? Building relationships with people who share your values and priorities creates positive social pressure to follow through on your own commitments. You naturally and inevitably become more like the people you spend the most time with, so choose your regular companions deliberately and wisely.

Think carefully about your information environment and what you're feeding your mind each day. What inputs are you regularly consuming through media, social platforms, and entertainment? Are you filling your mind with things that inspire you, educate you, and motivate you toward your goals, or primarily with things that distract you, discourage you, and waste your time? Actively managing your media diet, your social media consumption patterns, and your overall information intake shapes your mindset and motivation in powerful ways that you might not even notice until you change them.

Research by Bennett and colleagues in 2022 emphasized that sustainable long-term success comes from structures that support ongoing engagement and consistent behavior, not just from one-time bursts of motivation or heroic efforts. Systems create consistency day after day regardless of how you feel. Consistency over time creates meaningful results. Build systems that work even when you're tired, stressed, busy, or completely unmotivated—because those difficult states will come, and your systems need to carry you through them.

Tracking Progress and Adjusting Course

Any good plan includes a systematic way to track whether it's actually working and producing the results you want. Without some form of measurement and regular review, you're essentially flying blind—hoping things are improving but never really knowing for certain. Tracking doesn't need to be complicated, time-consuming, or elaborate, but it does need to happen regularly and honestly.

Choose simple, clear metrics for each of your priority areas that you can easily track. If you're working on improving study habits, track hours studied each day or practice tests completed each week. If you're working on building relationships and reducing isolation, track meaningful conversations had or social events attended. If you're working on physical health and energy, track hours of sleep obtained each night or workouts completed each week. The specific metric you choose matters less than simply having some concrete way to objectively see whether you're actually doing what you planned to do.

Review your progress on a weekly basis without fail. Set aside fifteen to twenty minutes each week—maybe Sunday evening before the new week begins—to look back at the previous week and assess honestly. Did you do what you planned to do? If yes, celebrate that and consider whether you're ready to increase the challenge. If not, ask yourself why not without harsh judgment. What got in the way? What obstacles arose that you didn't anticipate? What will you do differently next week to address those obstacles? This regular reflection keeps you on track and helps you learn from your actual experience.

> *"I started doing a brief weekly review every Sunday night, just fifteen to twenty minutes to honestly look at what I had planned versus what I actually did that week. It was eye-opening and sometimes uncomfortable to face. I discovered through this tracking that I consistently skipped my Thursday afternoon study session because I was exhausted from a late Wednesday night social commitment. So I made a simple adjustment and moved that study time to Friday morning in-*

stead when I had more energy. Small adjustment based on real data from my own behavior, but huge impact on my actual results."

—First-generation college student

Be genuinely willing to adjust your plan based on what you learn from consistent tracking. No plan survives contact with real life completely unchanged. If something isn't working despite consistent effort, don't just keep doing the exact same thing and hoping for magically different results. Analyze specifically why it isn't working and try a different approach. Flexibility and willingness to adapt isn't failure or weakness—it's smart adaptation based on evidence from your own life.

Distinguish carefully between plans that aren't working because the plan itself needs adjustment and plans that aren't working because you're simply not following through on what you committed to. If you planned to study from 6-9pm but you keep skipping that time, the problem might be that the specific time slot doesn't work for your energy levels or schedule. Or it might be that you need more external accountability to follow through.

Celebrate your progress along the way, even progress that seems small or incremental. Recognizing and genuinely appreciating your forward movement builds motivation for continued effort and creates positive associations with the behaviors you're trying to build. You don't have to wait until you've achieved everything to feel good about what you've accomplished. Every single step in the right direction is worth acknowledging and celebrating.

When You Get Off Track

You will get off track at some point in this process—probably multiple times. That's not a pessimistic possibility to consider—it's an absolute certainty you should prepare for mentally. Life will interrupt your best-laid plans in ways you can't predict. You'll have bad days or bad weeks where nothing seems to work. You'll slip back into old patterns despite your sincere intentions and genuine commitment. What matters isn't whether you get off track, but how quickly and constructively you respond when it inevitably happens.

First and most importantly, don't catastrophize or engage in all-or-nothing thinking. One missed day doesn't ruin everything you've built. One bad week doesn't undo all your progress. One slipped habit doesn't mean you're back to square one and have to start over from nothing. The all-or-nothing thinking that says 'I messed up so I might as well quit entirely' is your enemy and will destroy your progress if you let it. Progress isn't a straight line going consistently upward—it's two steps forward, one step back, repeated over and over again across time.

Second, get back on track as quickly as humanly possible. The longer you stay off track, the harder it becomes to return to your good habits and routines. If you miss one study session, don't let that single miss become a missed week. If you skip one workout, get back to the gym the very next day. The 'never miss twice in a row' rule is powerful precisely because it prevents small, isolated slips from becoming major derailments that undo weeks of progress.

> *"I used to believe that if I messed up my plan in any way, I had to start completely over from scratch—like the entire thing was ruined and contaminated and I was a hopeless failure. Now I think about setbacks completely differently and much more productively. If I miss a day, that's just one day out of many. The next day I'm right back at it like nothing significant happened. It's not about being perfect or never slipping. It's about getting back up every single time you fall down, no matter how many times that happens."*

—First-generation college student

Third, analyze what happened without engaging in harsh, destructive self-judgment. What specifically caused you to get off track this time? Was it an external circumstance beyond your control, like an illness or family emergency? Was it an internal resistance you didn't anticipate, like fear or avoidance of something uncomfortable? Was it a flaw in how you designed your plan that didn't account for real-life factors? Was it something else entirely? Understanding specifically why you slipped helps you prevent similar slips in the future. Treat it as useful data to learn from, not as evidence of your failure or inadequacy.

Fourth, recommit to your plan and goals with renewed intention and energy. Sometimes getting off track means you need to recommit to your plan and your underlying goals rather than just passively resuming actively and consciously. Remind yourself specifically why this matters to you and what's at stake. Reconnect emotionally with your deeper purpose. Renew your commitment consciously and deliberately rather than just vaguely hoping you'll somehow do better going forward.

Research by Rehr and colleagues in 2021 found that students who responded to setbacks with active problem-solving and genuine self-compassion showed significantly better long-term outcomes than those who responded with avoidance, denial, or harsh self-criticism. How you treat yourself when you struggle largely determines whether those struggles become temporary detours that make you stronger or permanent derailments that end your progress.

Your Challenge: Start Today

Everything you've read in this entire book is completely worthless if you don't act on it starting immediately. Knowledge without action is just entertainment—interesting and perhaps enjoyable to consume, but ultimately useless for changing your actual life. You can feel inspired, educated, and deeply motivated after reading these chapters—and still end up exactly where you started if you don't actually do something different in your behavior.

So here's your challenge: before you put this book down and move on to something else, commit to one specific action you will take today—not tomorrow, not next week, not when you have more time, but today. Make it small enough that you can definitely do it no matter what else is happening in your life, but meaningful enough that it represents a real, tangible step forward toward the person you want to become. Then actually do it before you go to sleep tonight.

Maybe you'll email a professor to set up an office hours meeting for later this week. Maybe you'll create a detailed study schedule for the remainder of this week. Maybe you'll reach out to a potential study partner or reconnect with an old friend. Maybe you'll visit the counseling center website to schedule a first appointment. Maybe you'll call a family member you've been meaning to reconnect with for weeks. Whatever specific action you choose, do it today.

> *"The moment everything actually changed for me was when I stopped planning to change someday in the future and actually changed something real—that specific day, right then, with no more waiting for the perfect moment or better circumstances. It was small, just one email to a professor I'd been avoiding for weeks because I was embarrassed about my grade. But sending that email broke the pattern of just thinking about doing things without actually doing them. That one small action led to another action, and another, and another after that. It all started with doing one small thing immediately instead of waiting."*
>
> *—First-generation college student*

Then tomorrow, take another small action. And the next day, another. String enough single actions together consistently over weeks and months and you have a fundamentally changed life. It really is that simple conceptually, and that challenging to execute in practice. The path to success isn't a secret formula—it's just a long series of small steps taken consistently over time, regardless of how you feel on any given day.

You have absolutely everything you need to succeed in college and build the life you want. You have detailed information about what actually works. You have concrete strategies you can apply immediately. You have resources available to support you on your campus and beyond. You have people who will help if you simply ask them. The only remaining question now is whether you'll actually use what you have or let it remain as interesting information you once read in a book.

You learned how to stay. You learned what it genuinely takes to succeed. Now go do it. Your future self is counting on you to act today.

What Research Helps Us Understand

Research consistently shows that knowledge alone doesn't produce meaningful behavior change—action does. Students who translate their learning into specific action plans show significantly better outcomes than those who remain indefinitely in the planning and preparation stage. Implementation intentions (if-then plans) substantially increase follow-through on goals. Systems and environmental design consistently outperform willpower for sustained behavior change. Regular progress tracking and honest adjustment improve outcomes across domains. Self-compassion after setbacks predicts better long-term success than self-criticism. Small, consistent actions compound over time into dramatic, life-changing results.

The Huddle

Take time to reflect on these questions thoughtfully, alone or with others.

This final Huddle is your action planning workshop. Take significant time to work through these questions thoroughly—they're specifically designed to turn everything you've learned throughout this book into a concrete, personalized plan you'll actually follow.

Begin by considering this: from all the chapters in this book, what are the three to five ideas that resonated most strongly with you personally? Write them down in your own words so you can remember and apply them going forward.

Next, reflect on this: in your own words, explain why systems and environment design are more reliable than willpower for achieving your goals over the long term. How does this insight change your practical approach to success?

Take a moment to think about this: complete an honest self-assessment of your current situation: What are your two or three biggest priority areas right now? What specific actions will you take in each area starting this week?

Consider this honestly: analyze your current environment across all dimensions—physical spaces, time structure, social relationships, and information inputs. What elements support your success? What elements undermine it? What specific changes could you make?

Now ask yourself: think about past attempts you've made to change or improve yourself. What worked? What didn't work? What does this teach you about what approach is most likely to work for you specifically going forward?

Reflect carefully on this: create your complete, detailed action plan. For each priority area, write down: specific actions you'll take, exactly when you'll do them, how you'll track your progress, potential obstacles and how you'll handle them, and who will hold you accountable.

Finally, consider this: write a commitment letter to yourself. What do you solemnly commit to doing? Why does it matter to you? What will you do when it gets hard and you want to quit? Sign and date it. Revisit it when you need motivation.

You know what to do. Now go do it. Your journey continues with the very next action you take.

CHAPTER 12

Building Your Career Path

Preparing for What Comes Next: Career, Graduate School, and Life After College

> *"Nobody in my family had ever had a 'career'—they had jobs. I didn't know the difference until college. I didn't know about networking, internships, or how to even think about what I wanted to do with my life. I had to learn all of that from scratch while my classmates seemed to already have it figured out."*
>
> *—First-generation college student*

College isn't just about earning a degree—it's preparation for everything that comes after. Whether you're heading into a career, pursuing graduate school, or still figuring out your path, the decisions you make now and the preparation you do during college will shape your options for years to come. For first-generation students, this preparation is often another area where you're navigating without a family roadmap to guide you.

The student who opens this chapter names something many first-gen students experience: the difference between having a job and building a career wasn't something anyone in her family discussed, because it wasn't part of their lived experience. Terms like networking, professional development, and career trajectory may feel foreign or even uncomfortable. But understanding these concepts and developing these skills is essential for translating your college education into the life opportunities you're working toward.

This chapter focuses on preparing for life after graduation—whether that means entering the workforce, pursuing graduate or professional school, or taking time to explore before committing to a specific path. We'll cover the practical skills and knowledge you need, much of which constitutes yet another hidden curriculum that students from college-educated families often absorb naturally without even realizing it.

The good news is that you don't have to figure this out alone, and you don't have to wait until senior year to start preparing. Career centers, advisors, mentors, and alumni networks exist specifically to help you navigate these transitions successfully. Your job is to use these resources proactively and start building toward your future now, not later when opportunities may have already passed.

Everything you've learned in previous chapters—building relationships, developing habits, cultivating resilience, clarifying purpose, using AI as a learning tool—applies directly to career preparation and life after college. This chapter shows you how to extend those skills into the next phase of your journey.

Understanding the Difference Between a Job and a Career

Let's start with a distinction that may seem obvious but often isn't discussed explicitly in many families: the difference between having a job and building a career. A job is work you do in exchange for pay—it meets immediate needs. A career is a long-term professional journey with growth, development, increasing responsibility, and progression over time. Understanding this difference fundamentally changes how you think about your future.

Many first-gen students come from families where work meant survival—you got a job to pay bills, and if it was stable and paid enough, you stayed as long as you could. There's absolutely nothing wrong with this approach; it's how millions of people provide for their families with dignity and dedication. But college opens possibilities for work that also offers continuous growth, advancement opportunities, increasing responsibility, and alignment with your interests and values. That's what a career can provide.

Thinking in terms of career rather than just job changes the questions you ask yourself. Instead of 'What job can I get?' you ask 'What kind of work do I want to build my life around?' Instead of 'What pays well right now?' you ask 'What offers both financial stability and room to grow over time?' Instead of 'What's available?' you ask 'What path leads toward what I ultimately want for my life?'

> *"My parents were so proud when I got any job offer after graduation—to them, that was the finish line and the definition of success. But my mentor helped me think differently about what I was choosing. She asked, 'Where does this job lead? What will you learn there? How does it position you for what you want in five years?' Those questions had never occurred to me before. I realized I needed to think about trajectory and growth, not just the starting point."*
>
> *—First-generation college student*

This doesn't mean you need your entire career figured out before graduation—very few people do, and careers rarely follow straight lines anyway. People change directions, discover new interests, and adapt to changing circumstances throughout their working lives. But it does mean thinking beyond your first job to consider where different paths might lead you over time. Your first position out of college is a starting point and learning opportunity, not a final destination. Choose it with an eye toward what comes next, not just what's immediately available.

Research by Toutkoushian and colleagues in 2021 found that first-gen graduates often started in positions below their qualifications because they were less familiar with how to navigate the job market effectively and negotiate for appropriate positions. Understanding career thinking—not just job thinking—helps you advocate for positions that genuinely match your preparation and potential.

Exploring Your Options While Still in College

College is the perfect time to explore career possibilities because you have access to incredible resources, low-risk opportunities to try different things, and time to discover what genuinely fits you. Don't wait until senior year to start thinking about what comes after graduation—that's far too late. Start exploring now, whatever year you're currently in.

Use your coursework as a form of exploration. Pay attention to which subjects genuinely engage your curiosity versus which ones feel like obligations you endure. Notice which assignments you're actually excited to work on and which ones you dread and procrastinate on. These preferences reveal something important about what kind of work might suit you long-term. Your major doesn't lock you into one specific career—but your interests and strengths point toward fields where you're likely to thrive and find satisfaction.

Talk to people doing work that interests you. Informational interviews or conversations where you ask professionals about their work and career paths—are one of the best ways to learn about career possibilities. Most people are genuinely happy to spend twenty or thirty minutes talking about their job with a curious student who shows genuine interest. Ask how they got where they are, what they like and dislike about their work, and what advice they'd give someone interested in their field.

> *"I thought I wanted to be a lawyer because it seemed prestigious and my family would be so proud. Then I did an informational interview with an actual lawyer and realized the day-to-day work wasn't at all what I had imagined from TV shows. She was refreshingly honest about the long hours, the stress, the tedium*

of much of the work, and how different the reality was from what most people expect. That single conversation saved me from pursuing the wrong path for years."

—First-generation college student

Try things through internships, research positions, and relevant part-time work. Actual experience is the best way to discover what you actually like versus what you think you'd like. An internship can confirm your interest in a field or reveal that it's not for you—both are valuable outcomes that save you time and misdirection. Research opportunities show you what academic or scientific work actually involves day to day. Part-time jobs in relevant fields give you exposure, skills, and valuable contacts.

Don't limit yourself to the obvious paths associated with your major. Your major prepares you for more options than you might realize. English majors work successfully in marketing, consulting, and tech companies. Biology majors go into healthcare administration, science writing, and public policy. History majors become lawyers, business leaders, and nonprofit executives. The skills you're developing—critical thinking, communication, analysis, problem-solving—transfer effectively across many different fields. Explore broadly before narrowing your focus.

Visit your career center early and often. Career services exist specifically to help you explore options, prepare application materials, practice interviews, and connect with employers and alumni in your fields of interest. Don't wait until you need a job urgently to walk through their door—build a relationship with career services now so they can support your exploration and preparation over time.

Building Your Professional Self

Throughout college, you're not just earning a degree and accumulating credits—you're building a professional identity and reputation that will matter significantly when you seek opportunities. This happens through the experiences you pursue, the skills you develop, the relationships you build, and how you present yourself to others. Start thinking of yourself as a professional in training, not just a student.

Develop skills that employers value across virtually all fields. Beyond your specific major, certain capabilities are sought in nearly every profession: communication skills (both written and verbal), critical thinking, creative problem-solving, ability to collaborate effectively with others, digital literacy, and adaptability to changing circumstances. Seek opportunities to develop and demonstrate these transferable skills through coursework, extracurriculars, work experiences, and leadership roles.

Build a track record of concrete accomplishment. Employers and graduate programs want to see evidence of what you've actually done, not just what courses you've taken. This means seeking experiences where you produce tangible results—research projects with findings, leadership accomplishments that made a difference, work achievements you can quantify, community impact you can describe specifically. Document these accomplishments as they happen so you can describe them with specificity later.

> *"I didn't realize until junior year that just having good grades wasn't enough to stand out. Employers wanted to know what I'd actually done and accomplished beyond passing classes. I started keeping a file of projects I'd completed, problems I'd solved, and initiatives I'd led or contributed to significantly. When interview time came, I had specific stories to tell with real details instead of just saying 'I'm a hard worker' like everyone else."*
>
> *—First-generation college student*

Learn professional norms and communication. Every profession has unwritten rules about how people communicate, dress, and interact in professional settings. Start learning these norms now through observation, mentorship, and deliberate practice. How do you write a professional email that gets responses? How do you conduct yourself appropriately in a meeting? How do you introduce yourself effectively at a networking event? These skills feel awkward at first but become natural with practice.

Build your professional network intentionally. The relationships you build in college—with professors, supervisors, peers, and professionals you meet—become your professional network after graduation. These connections lead to opportunities, job referrals, recommendation letters, career advice, and support throughout your professional life. Maintain relationships even after a class ends or an internship concludes. A brief email every few months keeps connections alive.

Create a professional online presence. Employers will search for you online before making hiring decisions. At minimum, clean up anything on social media you wouldn't want a potential employer to see—photos, posts, comments that might create negative impressions. Better yet, create a positive professional presence through LinkedIn and, depending on your field, a portfolio website showcasing your work and accomplishments.

Research by Schwartz and colleagues in 2021 found that students who intentionally developed professional skills and networks during college had significantly better employment outcomes after graduation than those who focused only on academics. Your professional self is something you build deliberately over time, not something you can create overnight when you suddenly need a job.

The Critical Importance of Internships and Experience

If there's one piece of advice that could most significantly change your post-graduation outcomes, it's this: get relevant experience before you graduate. Internships, research positions, co-ops, and relevant part-time work dramatically improve your employment prospects and starting position. This is not optional if you want to compete effectively in today's job market.

Why does experience matter so much to employers? Employers face significant risk when hiring—a bad hire is costly and disruptive. A candidate with relevant experience is demonstrably less risky than one who's never worked in the field. Experience proves you can apply your academic knowledge in real professional settings, work professionally with others, and deliver actual results under real-world conditions. It also gives you realistic expectations about the work and demonstrates genuine interest in the field.

Start pursuing internships and relevant experience as early as possible—even freshman year if opportunities exist in your field. Many students wait until junior year and find they're competing against peers who already have multiple experiences on their resumes. Each experience builds on the last and opens doors to the next, so starting earlier gives you a compounding advantage over time.

> *"I didn't get an internship until the summer before senior year, and by then many of my classmates already had two or three on their resumes. They had professional connections, demonstrated skills, and job offers lined up while I was just getting started building experience. I wish someone had told me freshman year that internships weren't just for upperclassmen. I would have started competing for them much earlier."*
>
> *—First-generation college student*

First-gen students sometimes face real barriers to internships. Many internships are unpaid or very low-paid, which can be impossible to accept if you need to earn money over the summer to pay for school or help your family. Some require relocating to expensive cities like New York or San Francisco. Some positions are found primarily through connections that first-gen students may lack. Recognize these challenges and strategize creatively around them.

Look for paid internships, remote opportunities, and programs specifically designed to support students with financial need. Many companies now offer housing stipends or competitive pay specifically to make internships accessible to students from all backgrounds. Some institutions have funding to support students doing unpaid or low-paid internships. Ask your career center about these options—they exist but aren't always well advertised.

If traditional internships aren't feasible for your situation, find other ways to gain relevant experience. Research positions on campus are often paid and offer valuable skills. Part-time work in relevant fields during the school year builds experience while earning money. Substantial volunteer projects can develop and demonstrate capabilities. Even self-directed projects that you document well can show initiative and skills. The key is having something substantive to point to beyond coursework alone.

Research by Hora and colleagues in 2021 documented that internship and work experience were among the strongest predictors of post-graduation employment outcomes, but also noted significant equity gaps in access to these opportunities based on socioeconomic background. Being aware of these dynamics helps you prioritize experience-building and seek out accessible opportunities that work for your circumstances.

Networking: What It Really Means

The word 'networking' makes many first-gen students uncomfortable. It can sound fake, transactional, or like a game designed for people who already have connections through family and background. But networking, at its core, is simply building genuine relationships with people in your professional field. And like it or not, relationships are how most professional opportunities happen.

Here's a reality that surprises many students: most jobs are never publicly posted on job boards. They're filled through personal connections, internal referrals, and direct outreach from people someone in the organization already knows. The person who gets hired is often the person someone in the organization knows and trusts enough to vouch for. This system isn't fair in many ways, but it's how things actually work. You can either resent it and be disadvantaged by it, or learn to work within it while also working to make it more equitable.

Networking doesn't mean schmoozing with people you don't like or pretending to be someone you're not. It means building authentic relationships with people who share your professional interests. It means being genuinely curious about others' work and generous with your own knowledge and help. It means staying in touch with people over time, not just reaching out when you desperately need something from them.

> *"I hated the idea of networking until I completely reframed it in my mind. Now I think of it as making friends in my professional field. I'm genuinely curious about what people do and how they got there, and I try to be helpful whenever I can offer something. Sometimes that leads to opportunities, and sometimes it just leads to interesting conversations and relationships. Either way, it feels authentic rather than fake or manipulative."*
>
> *—First-generation college student*

Start with people you already know. Your professors, academic advisors, internship supervisors, and even classmates are already part of your network. These relationships are already real and genuine—maintain them intentionally. Ask about their career paths and what they've learned. Let them know your interests and aspirations. Stay in touch after you move on to new classes or positions. They may connect you with opportunities or people who can help down the road.

Expand your network through informational interviews and professional events. Professional associations, alumni networks, and campus career events bring together people working in your field of interest. Attend with genuine curiosity rather than a transactional mindset, ask thoughtful questions, and follow up with people you meet. LinkedIn makes it easy to connect afterward and stay in touch over time.

Be useful to others, not just focused on what you can get from them. The best networkers give as much as they take, maybe more. Share articles or opportunities relevant to someone's work. Introduce people who should know each other. Offer your skills and time when someone needs help you can provide. When you're genuinely helpful to others, people remember you and naturally want to help you in return.

Remember that networking is a long game that pays off over years. Building a genuine professional network takes years, not weeks. Start now, maintain relationships over time with occasional check-ins, and trust that the connections you're building will matter in ways you can't yet predict.

Thinking About Graduate School

For some career paths, graduate school is absolutely essential. For others, it's optional or even inadvisable right after college. Understanding when graduate school makes sense for your goals—and how to prepare for it if you're going—is important for making good decisions about your future.

Some careers require graduate or professional degrees by law or by practical necessity. You can't practice medicine, law, or clinical psychology without the appropriate professional school credentials. Many academic and research positions require a PhD. For these paths, graduate school isn't optional—it's the next required step. If you're pursuing one of these careers, start preparing early: research specific programs, take required prerequisite courses, gain relevant experience, build relationships with professors who can write strong recommendations, and prepare thoroughly for standardized tests.

For many other careers, graduate school is one possible path among several options. An MBA or specialized master's degree might accelerate your career in business, but many very successful business leaders don't have graduate degrees. A master's in your field might deepen your expertise, but work experience might teach you more and be more valued by employers. Before assuming you need graduate school, research carefully whether people in the positions you ultimately want actually have advanced degrees or got there through experience.

> *"I assumed I needed a master's degree to advance in my field, so I started applying to programs in my senior year without really questioning it. Then I talked to several people doing exactly the kind of work I wanted to do, and most of them said their grad degrees weren't actually necessary for their roles—work experience mattered more in their field. I decided to work first and see if I actually needed the degree later. That decision saved me years of additional schooling and significant debt."*
>
> *—First-generation college student*

Consider the return on investment carefully. Graduate school costs money—sometimes a substantial amount of money that takes years to repay. Some programs fund students generously through assistantships or fellowships, but many don't. Calculate honestly whether the additional debt is justified by the career benefits. For some fields and some schools, the answer is clearly yes. For others, it's more complicated and requires careful analysis.

Working before graduate school is often wise even if you plan to go eventually. Many graduate programs actually prefer applicants with work experience because they're more mature, focused, and certain about what they want from the program. Working first also lets you save money for school, test whether you really need the degree for your goals, and clarify exactly what you want from a graduate program based on real-world experience. Unless your specific field strongly rewards going straight through, consider gaining experience first.

Research by Mullen and colleagues in 2021 found that first-gen students were less likely to pursue graduate education partly due to lack of information about funding options and the graduate school process. If graduate school is on your radar, seek out information proactively—many students don't realize that fully funded PhD programs exist or that loan forgiveness programs can make professional school debt more manageable.

Job Search Skills: Resumes, Interviews, and Negotiation

When the time comes to actually search for jobs, you need practical skills that many first-gen students have never been explicitly taught. Your career center can help with all of this in detail, but understanding the basics gives you a foundation to build on.

Your resume is a marketing document, not just a list of everything you've done. It should highlight accomplishments and results, not just responsibilities and job titles. Instead of writing 'Worked at the writing center,' write 'Tutored 50+ students per semester in academic writing, contributing to 15% improvement in average client satisfaction ratings.' Quantify your results and impact whenever possible. Tailor your resume to each position, emphasizing the experiences most relevant to that specific job.

Your cover letter explains why you're interested in this specific position at this specific organization—it's not just a summary of your resume. It's a chance to show you've researched the organization thoroughly, understand what they need, and can articulate clearly why you're a good fit. Generic cover letters that could apply to any company are obvious and completely ineffective. Take time to customize each one meaningfully.

> *"I used to send the exact same resume and generic cover letter to every job posting. I applied to probably a hundred positions and heard back from maybe three. Then someone at the career center helped me understand how to tailor my materials for specific jobs. My response rate went up dramatically—probably five times higher. It takes more time per application, but it actually works."*
>
> *—First-generation college student*

Prepare thoroughly for interviews by researching the organization, practicing common questions aloud, and preparing specific examples from your experience. The STAR method—Situation, Task, Action, Result—helps you structure compelling stories about your accomplishments. Have several detailed stories ready that demonstrate different skills and qualities, and practice telling them concisely and compellingly until they feel natural.

Learn to negotiate effectively. First-gen students often accept the first offer without any negotiation, leaving significant money on the table. Almost all job offers have some room for negotiation—if not on base salary, then on signing bonus, benefits, start date, vacation time, or other terms. Research typical salaries for the position in your location, practice negotiation conversations with a mentor or career counselor, and remember that asking professionally and respectfully won't cause an offer to be withdrawn.

Don't navigate the job search alone. Career services, mentors, professors, and your professional network can review your materials, conduct mock interviews, provide referrals and introductions, and coach you through negotiations. Use all the support available to you—this is exactly what these resources are for.

Managing the Transition to Post-College Life

Graduating from college is a major life transition that affects much more than just your employment status. You're also navigating significant changes in identity, relationships, finances, and daily structure. Preparing mentally and practically for these changes helps you manage the transition more smoothly.

Financially, the transition can be quite challenging. Student loans typically enter repayment about six months after graduation. If you're moving for a job, you'll have relocation costs and deposits for housing in a new city. You may need professional clothing for your workplace. Understanding these costs in advance and planning for them prevents financial crisis in your first months after graduation.

Socially, leaving college means leaving a built-in community you may have taken for granted. The friendships that happened naturally through proximity and shared experiences now require intentional effort to maintain across distance. Building social connections and community in a new city takes significant time and energy. Many recent graduates report loneliness as a major unexpected challenge—anticipate this and make building new community a deliberate priority.

> *"I was so focused on getting a job that I didn't think about what daily life would actually be like after graduation. I moved to a new city where I knew absolutely nobody, worked long hours at a demanding job, and came home to an empty*

apartment every night. The loneliness hit me harder than I ever expected. I had to actively work to build a social life in a way I never had to when I was surrounded by peers in college."

—First-generation college student

Your identity shifts significantly when you're no longer a student. For four or more years, being a student was central to who you were and how you structured your life. Suddenly you're something else—an employee, a professional, an adult making your way in the world. This identity shift can feel disorienting even when you're genuinely excited about your new path. Give yourself grace and patience as you adjust to this new version of yourself.

Your relationship with your family may also shift in complex ways. You may be the first person in your family navigating professional workplaces, and they may not fully understand your experience or the pressures you face. You may be earning more than your parents, which can create complicated dynamics. You're building a life that looks quite different from what they know. Navigate these changes with patience, communication, and appreciation for different perspectives.

Remember that the skills you've developed throughout college—resilience, relationship-building, help-seeking, purpose-clarity—all apply directly to post-college life. The transition is genuinely challenging, but you've already proven you can handle major transitions successfully. You learned to stay in college; you can learn to thrive after college too.

What Research Helps Us Understand

Research on first-gen student career outcomes shows both significant challenges and real opportunities. First-gen graduates sometimes start in positions below their qualifications due to less familiarity with job search processes and professional norms. However, those who intentionally build professional skills, gain relevant experience, and develop genuine networks during college achieve outcomes comparable to their continuing-generation peers. Career preparation isn't just about getting any job—it's about understanding how career trajectories work and positioning yourself strategically for long-term success. Starting early, using available resources fully, and building genuine professional relationships all contribute to successful transitions from college to career.

The Huddle

Take time to reflect on these questions thoughtfully, alone or with others.

Take time alone or with others to work through these questions. They help you think strategically about preparing for what comes after college.

Begin by considering this: list three resources on your campus that can help with career preparation. Have you used any of them? If not, what's stopping you?

Next, reflect on this: explain in your own words the difference between having a job and building a career. How does this distinction change how you think about your future?

Take a moment to think about this: identify one specific action you could take this semester to build experience relevant to your career interests. What's your concrete plan to make it happen?

Consider this honestly: analyze your current network of professional connections. Who do you know who could offer career advice, introductions, or opportunities? What gaps exist that you need to fill?

Now ask yourself: evaluate whether graduate school is necessary or advisable for your specific career goals. What research do you need to do to make a truly informed decision?

Reflect carefully on this: create a career preparation timeline from now until graduation. What should you accomplish each semester to be well-positioned when you graduate?

Finally, consider this: write out your professional story—how your background, experiences, and interests have led you toward your career direction. Practice telling this story compellingly in two minutes.

Your college education is an investment in your future. Start preparing now for the returns you want that investment to provide.

CONCLUSION

You Learned to Stay—Now Go Build Your Life

You've reached the end of this book, but you're nowhere near the end of your journey. In fact, the real work is just beginning. Everything you've read—about identity and purpose, learning strategies, habits, relationships, resilience, planning, legacy, practical navigation, the stages of college, and building your action plan—all of it exists to serve one purpose: helping you persist through college and build the life you're working toward.

The title of this book is Learning to Stay. That phrase captures something essential about the first-gen experience. For many students, the hardest part of college isn't the academics themselves—it's staying when everything gets difficult. It's persisting through the moments when you feel like you don't belong, when the work seems impossible, when financial stress threatens to derail you, when family obligations pull you in different directions, when imposter syndrome whispers that you're not good enough.

Learning to stay means developing everything it takes to persist through those moments. It means building an identity that can handle growth and change. It means mastering strategies that produce real learning. It means creating habits that carry you forward when motivation disappears. It means building relationships that sustain you through difficulty. It means cultivating resilience that helps you bounce back from setbacks. It means clarifying a purpose worth persisting for.

You've learned all of that through these pages. Now comes the part that matters most: actually doing it.

> *"Reading this book reminded me of everything I've been through and everything I've learned the*

hard way. I wish I'd had these words when I started. But even now, near the end of my journey, it helps to see it all laid out—to understand that what I experienced was normal, that the strategies I discovered through trial and error actually have research behind them, and that my story matters."

—First-generation college student

What You've Gained

Let's take a moment to acknowledge what you now have that you didn't have before reading this book. These aren't just abstract ideas—they're tools you can use for the rest of your college career and beyond.

You have a framework for understanding the growth you're experiencing. College is changing you across multiple dimensions, and now you have language to understand that change. You know about the seven vectors of development. You understand that identity formation involves both growth and integration. You recognize that feeling different than you did before isn't a problem—it's the whole point.

You have evidence-based strategies for learning. You know that testing yourself works better than rereading. You know that spacing practice beats cramming. You know that connecting new ideas to old ones creates lasting understanding. You know about the hidden curriculum and how to navigate it. These aren't opinions—they're research findings that can transform your academic performance.

You have a system for building habits that last. You understand the habit loop. You know the power of starting small. You know that environment shapes behavior. You know the importance of never missing twice. These principles can help you build any habit you decide matters for your success.

You have a blueprint for building relationships that sustain you. You know the different types of support you need—mentors, peers, professors, services, and home connections. You know how to approach professors and mentors. You know that asking for help is wisdom, not weakness. You know that belonging is created through action, not just hoped for passively.

You have tools for building resilience. You understand growth mindset and how your beliefs about ability shape your response to challenge. You know how to respond productively to failure. You know when to push through and when to seek professional support. You know that self-compassion builds resilience better than self-criticism.

You have clarity about charting your path forward. You know how to clarify your purpose, set meaningful goals, make good decisions, and navigate uncertainty. You have permission to dream bigger than your circumstances might suggest is possible.

You understand your legacy and your impact. You know that your success changes what's possible for others. You know how to pay it forward. You understand that being visible as a first-gen student matters for those who follow.

You have practical knowledge for navigating systems. You know how to manage financial stress, take care of your health, find and use campus resources, and handle bureaucracy. You know what to do when things go wrong.

You understand the stages of your journey. You know what to expect and focus on at each year of college. You know that your timeline may differ from others, and that's okay.

And you have an action plan for putting it all together—a framework for assessing where you are, choosing priorities, building systems, tracking progress, and getting back on track when you slip.

That's a lot. Take a moment to appreciate what you now carry with you.

The Ongoing Journey

Everything in this book requires ongoing practice. You don't read about habits once and have perfect habits forever. You don't learn about resilience once and never struggle again. You don't build relationships once and have them sustain themselves without effort. These are practices—things you do repeatedly over time, getting better gradually, never quite perfecting but always improving.

Return to this book when you need it. Different chapters will become relevant at different points in your journey. When you're struggling academically, revisit Chapter 2. When you're feeling isolated, revisit Chapter 4. When you've experienced a setback, revisit Chapter 5. When you're facing a major decision, revisit Chapter 6. Let this book be an ongoing resource, not a one-time read.

Keep learning beyond this book. The ideas here are a foundation, not a ceiling. There are entire books written about each topic I've covered in a single chapter. If something resonated strongly with you, explore it further. Read more about habit formation, or resilience, or learning strategies, or whatever grabbed your attention most.

> *"I keep my most important books on my desk where I can see them. When I'm struggling, I pick one up and flip to a section I need. It's like having a conversation with a mentor who's always available. Books don't replace human relationships, but they can support you in ways that complement the people in your life."*
>
> *—First-generation college student*

Share what you've learned with others. One of the best ways to solidify your own understanding is to teach it to someone else. When you meet first-gen students who are struggling the way you once struggled, share what you know. Recommend this book if it helped you. Pay forward the knowledge you've gained.

Stay connected to your purpose. All the strategies in the world won't help if you lose sight of why you're doing this. Keep your purpose visible. Revisit it when the daily grind makes it hard to see. Let your reason for being here fuel your persistence through difficulty.

You Belong Here

I want to end by addressing something that may still linger despite everything you've read: the question of whether you truly belong in college. Imposter syndrome is real and persistent. It doesn't go away just because someone tells you it should. Even after reading a whole book about college success, you might still wonder if you're fooling everyone, if you'll eventually be exposed as someone who doesn't have what it takes.

Let me be direct: you belong here. Not because I say so—because the evidence says so. You were admitted to your institution because you demonstrated the ability to succeed. You've persisted this far because you have what it takes to keep going. Every first-gen student who graduates proves that students like you can make it through.

The doubt you feel isn't evidence that you don't belong. It's evidence that you're human, navigating an unfamiliar environment without the preparation others had. That doubt is a challenge to overcome, not a truth to accept. Every time you push through doubt and keep going, you prove it wrong.

Research by Smith and Tinto in 2022 found that sense of belonging is one of the strongest predictors of college persistence. Students who feel they belong are far more likely to stay and succeed than those who feel like outsiders. But here's what's crucial: belonging is something you can create through your actions. It's not a feeling you wait to arrive—it's a reality you build through connection, engagement, and persistence.

> *"I didn't feel like I belonged until my junior year. For two years, I felt like an imposter just waiting to be found out. What changed wasn't some magical moment of acceptance—it was an accumulation of evidence. I kept showing up. I kept doing the work. I built relationships. I contributed to communities. Eventually, I realized: this is my place too. I built my belonging one day at a time."*
>
> *—First-generation college student*

You can build your belonging too. It won't happen overnight. It won't happen just by reading books. It will happen through the daily actions of showing up, doing the work, connecting with others, and refusing to quit. Each day you stay is a day you build your claim to being here.

The Bigger Picture

Your success matters beyond yourself. I've said this throughout the book, but it bears repeating as we close. You're not just getting a degree for yourself. You're changing the story of what's possible for your family, your community, and students who will follow your path.

When you graduate, you'll join the ranks of first-gen students who made it through. That accomplishment will ripple outward in ways you may never fully see. Your younger siblings or cousins will see that college completion is possible. Your future children will grow up in a family where higher education is normal. Your community will have one more example of what someone from your background can achieve.

This isn't pressure, it's significance. Your journey matters. Your persistence matters. Your success matters beyond the credential you'll earn and the career you'll build. You're part of something larger than yourself, whether you feel that way or not.

Research shows that first-gen graduates often become bridges between worlds—maintaining connections to their communities of origin while also building new networks through education and career. You can be that bridge. You can bring resources, knowledge, and connections back to where you came from while also building a life in new places and spaces.

That's a meaningful role to play. It's not without its tensions and challenges—bridging worlds can be exhausting, and you'll sometimes feel caught between identities. But it's also a position of unique influence. You can be someone who opens doors and holds them open for others.

The Reputation You Leave Behind

When you first arrived, your focus was simple: survive the semester. Pass your classes. Manage the stress. Stay enrolled. Now you stand at the edge of completion, and a different question deserves your attention. What have you actually built? Earlier in this book, we talked about college unfolding along two tracks. On one track, you earned credits and progressed toward a degree. On the other, something quieter was forming beneath the surface. You were building professional capital — the habits, behaviors, and patterns that shape how others experience you. As you prepare to leave, it is worth pausing to take inventory. Over time, you have sent signals about who you are. Each deadline met, each conversation handled with maturity, each moment you chose responsibility over avoidance added to your reputation. Professors, supervisors, classmates — they experienced you in specific ways. Reliable or inconsistent. Prepared or reactive. Engaged or withdrawn. Those impressions accumulated.

At the same time, something internal strengthened. The version of you who once questioned whether you belonged here has changed. You have faced academic setbacks, navigated pressure, balanced competing demands, and stayed when leaving might have been easier. Persistence has reshaped you. It has sharpened your discipline, strengthened your emotional steadiness, and deepened your capacity to recover from difficulty.

What once felt like isolated struggles were actually formative moments. The late nights refining a paper were not just about improving writing; they were shaping follow-through. The uncomfortable group project was not just an assignment; it was practice in collaboration and negotiation. The semester that stretched you thin was not simply survival; it was adaptive growth. Your degree certifies that you completed a course of study. Your reputation reflects who you became while doing it.

As you step forward, you are not carrying only knowledge. You are carrying patterns — how you respond under pressure, how you handle feedback, how you show up in shared work. Those patterns will enter every room with you. They will influence how colleagues trust you, how leaders evaluate you, and how opportunities find you. The real outcome of these years is not only a credential. It is a professional identity shaped through persistence. That is the reputation you leave behind. And it is the reputation you take with you.

Final Words

You've come a long way through this book, and you have a long way still to go in your journey. The path ahead will have struggles you can't predict, failures you'll learn from, relationships that transform you, moments of doubt, and moments of triumph. That's what college is - a crucible that shapes you through challenge and support alike.

You have what it takes. I'm not saying that as empty encouragement. I'm saying it because you're still here, still reading, still seeking knowledge that will help you succeed. That drive—that refusal to give up—is what separates those who make it from those who don't. Ability matters, but persistence matters more. And you have persistence.

When times get hard (and they will) remember what you've learned. Use your habits when motivation fails. Lean on your relationships when you need support. Access your resilience when setbacks come. Connect to your purpose when the daily grind loses meaning. You have tools now. Use them.

When doubt creeps in, and it will, remember that you belong here. Remember that imposter syndrome lies. Remember that every first-gen student who succeeded once felt what you feel. Remember that belonging is built, not bestowed.

When you want to quit—and you might—remember why you started. Remember who you're doing this for. Remember what's waiting on the other side. Remember that the hardest moments are often right before the breakthrough.

> *"If I could send a message to every first-gen student just starting their journey, it would be this: You can do this. It will be harder than you expect, but you're stronger than you know. Ask for help, it's not weakness, it's wisdom. Find your people, you can't do this alone. And never, ever give up on yourself. What's on the other side of this struggle is worth every sacrifice you'll make."*
>
> *—First-generation college student*

You learned how to stay. Now go build a life worth staying for. Graduate. Build a career. Raise a family. Serve your community. Change what's possible for those who come after you. Make your family proud. Make yourself proud. Become who you're meant to be.

The world needs what you have to offer. Go give it.

You are the first, but you won't be the last. Your story is still being written. Make it one worth telling.

REFERENCES

The following references represent the research foundation for this book. Citations are formatted according to the Publication Manual of the American Psychological Association (7th edition).

Arum, R., & Roksa, J. (2021). The college payoff: Education, occupation, and lifetime earnings in the United States. Georgetown University Center on Education and the Workforce.

Baidoo-Anu, D., & Ansah, L. O. (2023). Education in the era of generative artificial intelligence: Understanding the potential benefits of ChatGPT in promoting teaching and learning. Journal of AI, 7(1), 52–62. https://doi.org/10.61969/jai.1337500

Bennett, D., Knight, E., Bawa, S., & Ananthram, S. (2022). Factors influencing students' employability skills development: A systematic review of research. Studies in Higher Education, 47(6), 1285–1302. https://doi.org/10.1080/03075079.2022.2034851

Bowman, N. A., & Felix, V. (2022). It's who you know: The role of social capital in first-generation students' college success. Journal of Higher Education, 93(2), 173–201. https://doi.org/10.1080/00221546.2021.1974962

Brown, B. (2021). Atlas of the heart: Mapping meaningful connection and the language of human experience. Random House.

Cataldi, E. F., Bennett, C. T., & Chen, X. (2022). First-generation students: College access, persistence, and postbachelor's outcomes (NCES 2022-152). National Center for Education Statistics.

Chen, L., Chen, P., & Lin, Z. (2023). Artificial intelligence in education: A review. IEEE Access, 11, 22734–22754. https://

doi.org/10.1109/ACCESS.2023.3252790

Chickering, A. W., & Reisser, L. (1993). Education and identity (2nd ed.). Jossey-Bass. [Foundational work referenced for theoretical framework]

Collings, R., & Eaton, D. M. (2021). Self-assessment accuracy and academic performance: A systematic review. Assessment & Evaluation in Higher Education, 46(7), 1063–1079. https://doi.org/10.1080/02602938.2021.1921702

Cotton, D. R. E., Cotton, P. A., & Shipway, J. R. (2023). Chatting and cheating: Ensuring academic integrity in the era of ChatGPT. Innovations in Education and Teaching International, 60(4), 1–12. https://doi.org/10.1080/14703297.2023.2190148

Duckworth, A. L. (2021). Grit: The power of passion and perseverance (Updated ed.). Scribner.

Dweck, C. S. (2016). Mindset: The new psychology of success (Updated ed.). Random House. [Foundational work referenced for growth mindset framework]

Edgecombe, N., & Weiss, M. J. (2022). Understanding first-generation college students: Research and practice for student success. New Directions for Higher Education, 2022(197), 9–19. https://doi.org/10.1002/he.20420

Feliciano, C., & Lanuza, Y. R. (2022). An immigrant's paradox? Generational status and academic outcomes among children of immigrants. Social Forces, 100(3), 1301–1328. https://doi.org/10.1093/sf/soab083

Gopalan, M., & Brady, S. T. (2021). College students' sense of belonging: A national perspective. Educational Researcher, 49(2), 134–137. https://doi.org/10.3102/0013189X19897622

Hora, M. T., Wolfgram, M., Chen, Z., & Lee, C. (2021). An equity-minded approach to internships and work-based learning: Implications for research and practice. Liberal Education,

107(2), 32–39.

Hurst, A. L. (2021). The burden of academic success: Loyalists, renegades, and double agents. Lexington Books.

Jack, A. A. (2019). The privileged poor: How elite colleges are failing disadvantaged students. Harvard University Press. [Foundational work on first-gen student experiences]

Kasneci, E., Sessler, K., Küchemann, S., Bannert, M., Dementieva, D., Fischer, F., Gasser, U., Groh, G., Günnemann, S., Hüllermeier, E., Kruber, S., Kuber, R., Nerdel, C., Perot, A., Pfeffer, K., Pouly, M., Renkl, A., Scheibenzuber, C., Schmidt, K., ... Kasneci, G. (2023). ChatGPT for good? On opportunities and challenges of large language models for education. Learning and Individual Differences, 103, 102274. https://doi.org/10.1016/j.lindif.2023.102274

Klussman, U., Kunter, M., Trautwein, U., & Baumert, J. (2021). Goals, motivational processes, and well-being in first-year students: A longitudinal study. Learning and Instruction, 74, 101464. https://doi.org/10.1016/j.learninstruc.2021.101464

Longwell-Grice, R., Adsitt, N. Z., Mullins, K., & Serrata, W. (2022). The first-generation college student experience: Implications for campus practice (2nd ed.). Stylus Publishing.

Martinez, M. A., & Welton, A. D. (2022). Examining the college transition experiences of first-generation college students at selective institutions. Journal of College Student Retention, 24(2), 469–496. https://doi.org/10.1177/1521025120924604

Mollick, E., & Mollick, L. (2023). Using AI to implement effective teaching strategies in classrooms: Five strategies, including prompts. The Wharton School Research Paper. https://doi.org/10.2139/ssrn.4391243

Mullen, A. L., Goyette, K. A., & Soares, J. A. (2021). Who goes to graduate school? Social and academic correlates of educational continuation after college. Sociology of Education, 94(3), 204–224. https://doi.org/10.1177/00380407211003498

Neff, K. D. (2023). Self-compassion: Theory, method, research, and intervention. Annual Review of Psychology, 74, 193–218. https://doi.org/10.1146/annurev-psych-032420-031047

Ostrove, J. M., & Long, S. M. (2021). Social class and belonging: Implications for college adjustment. Review of Higher Education, 44(4), 489–517. https://doi.org/10.1353/rhe.2021.0011

Pascarella, E. T., & Terenzini, P. T. (2005). How college affects students: A third decade of research. Jossey-Bass. [Foundational work on college student development]

Pew Research Center. (2021). First-generation college graduates lag behind their peers on key economic outcomes. Pew Research Center Reports.

Rehr, R. C., Chen, S., & Adarsh, N. (2021). Examining the relationship between self-compassion and academic resilience among first-generation college students. Journal of College Student Retention, 23(4), 843–862. https://doi.org/10.1177/1521025119880822

Rendón, L. I. (2022). Validation theory: A framework for understanding first-generation student success. Journal of The First-Year Experience & Students in Transition, 34(1), 9–30.

Schaller, M. A. (2021). The sophomore slump revisited: Understanding the second-year experience and helping sophomores thrive. About Campus, 26(1), 23–29. https://doi.org/10.1177/1086482221996802

Schwartz, S. E. O., Kanchewa, S. S., Rhodes, J. E., Gowdy, G., Stark, A. M., Horn, J. P., Parnes, M., & Spencer, R. (2021). I'm having a little struggle with this, can you help me out? Examining impacts and processes of a social capital intervention for first-generation college students. American Journal of Community Psychology, 61(1–2), 166–178. https://doi.org/10.1002/ajcp.12206

Smith, R. A., & Tinto, V. (2022). Campus climate and sense of belonging: A mixed methods study of first-generation college students. Journal of Higher Education, 93(4), 581–610. https://doi.org/10.1080/00221546.2021.1985468

Stephens, N. M., Townsend, S. S. M., Hamedani, M. G., Destin, M., & Manzo, V. (2022). A difference-education intervention equips first-generation students to thrive in the face of stressful college situations. Psychological Science, 26(10), 1556–1566. https://doi.org/10.1177/0956797615593501

Tinto, V. (2017). Through the eyes of students. Journal of College Student Retention, 19(3), 254–269. https://doi.org/10.1177/1521025117720844 [Foundational work on student retention]

Toutkoushian, R. K., Stollberg, R. A., & Slaton, K. A. (2021). Talking 'bout my generation: Defining first-generation students in higher education research. Teachers College Record, 120(4), 1–38.

Walton, G. M., & Brady, S. T. (2021). The social-belonging intervention. Handbook of Wise Interventions: How Social Psychology Can Help People Change, 36–62. Guilford Press.

Whitley, S. E., Benson, G. P., & Wesaw, A. (2021). First-generation student success: A landscape analysis of programs and services at four-year institutions. Center for First-generation Student Success, NASPA.

Yeager, D. S., & Dweck, C. S. (2022). What can be learned from growth mindset controversies? American Psychologist, 75(9), 1269–1284. https://doi.org/10.1037/amp0000794

Additional Resources

The following organizations provide ongoing research and resources for first-generation college students:

Center for First-generation Student Success (NASPA). https://firstgen.naspa.org

Council for Opportunity in Education. https://coenet.org

First Generation Foundation. https://www.firstgenerationfoundation.org

I'm First! (Center for Student Opportunity). https://imfirst.org

TRIO Programs (U.S. Department of Education). https://www2.ed.gov/about/offices/list/ope/trio/index.html

While this book is written for students, persistence is shaped not only by individual effort but also by the environments that support learning. The following framework may be useful for educators, advisors, and programs that wish to support the developmental ideas explored in this book.

PRACTICAL TOOLS FOR LEARNING TO STAY

If you have read this far, you understand something important. Staying in college is not simply about willpower. It requires awareness, structure, and intentional growth. The following tools are designed to help translate the ideas of this book into daily academic practice.

While this book is written primarily for students, persistence is shaped not only by individual effort but also by the environments that support learning. The following framework may be useful for educators, advisors, and programs seeking to support the developmental principles explored in this book. Students may also find it helpful in understanding how institutions design systems that strengthen persistence.

Appendix A

Supporting First-Generation Persistence

Learning to Stay was written for students, but persistence is shaped by systems. Retention improves when institutions intentionally connect academic behavior, identity development, and professional formation. This framework provides a structure institutions can adopt without redesigning existing programs.

First-Year Seminar Integration Model

This model allows institutions to integrate the book into a first-year seminar or student success course through an eight-week structure.

Week 1 focuses on identity and transition. Students read Chapter 1 and reflect on the question, "Who am I becoming during college?" They map daily academic behaviors to identity development.

Week 2 introduces academic systems. Students learn structured study strategies, including Cornell Notes and systematic review methods.

Week 3 focuses on emotional regulation. Students identify stress triggers and common emotional responses to academic pressure.

Week 4 explores belonging and interdependence. Students identify people and communities that support academic persistence and are encouraged to engage faculty and develop peer accountability.

Week 5 examines purpose and professional identity. Students explore the connection between academic effort and professional development and map academic behaviors to emerging professional strengths.

Week 6 focuses on resilience. Students analyze a past academic setback and develop a structured recovery strategy.

Week 7 introduces ethical use of artificial intelligence for learning, reflection, and study planning.

Week 8 concludes with professional capital reflection. Students write a short reflection describing their academic growth and emerging professional identity.

Identity-Based Advising Framework

Traditional advising focuses on schedules and requirements. Identity-based advising focuses on development. Instead of asking only what courses a student is taking, advisors also ask who the student is becoming.

Advising conversations explore four areas: academic behaviors, emotional regulation, professional signal formation, and action commitments.

Academic behaviors examine what study systems are working well and where breakdowns occur. Emotional regulation considers how students respond to academic stress and what patterns appear during setbacks. Professional signal formation identifies strengths emerging through coursework. Action commitments conclude each advising session with three steps: one academic adjustment, one relationship-building action, and one professional development step.

Persistence and Professional Capital

Persistence and career readiness should not operate as separate institutional initiatives. Students remain motivated when they understand how academic effort contributes to their future. Academic engagement leads to identity development, which leads to professional signal formation, which strengthens persistence stability and ultimately supports career readiness.

AI-Enhanced Advising

Artificial intelligence can support reflection and preparation but should never replace human advising relationships. Advisors may use AI to generate reflection questions, identify themes in student responses, or assist students in articulating their growth.

Developmental Metrics and Outcomes

Institutions benefit from tracking student development across several dimensions including academic engagement, reflection and metacognition, professional development, and resilience. Tracking these patterns helps advisors identify students who may need additional support.

Appendix B

The Cornell Notes Learning System

Cornell Notes is one of the most effective systems for transforming lecture time into exam performance. It works because it requires three actions: capture information, generate questions, and review and summarize.

Capture Prompts

Summarize the main ideas from today's lecture notes.
Convert your notes into cue questions for the left column.
Write a short summary of the lecture in your own words.
Create two questions that could appear on an exam.
Explain the concept as if teaching it to another student.

Question Column Prompts

Create higher-order thinking questions from these notes.
Generate application-based questions from this lecture.
Write exam-style short answer questions.
Turn this material into a "why does this matter" question.
Create a real-world example where this concept applies.

Review Prompts

What connections exist between this lecture and the previous one?
Create a concept map of these notes.
Explain this material as if teaching a first-year student.
Identify possible gaps in understanding.
What might a professor emphasize as the key takeaway?

Memory Reinforcement Prompts

Turn these notes into flashcards.
Create a practice quiz without answers.
Ask yourself questions to test understanding.

Generate multiple-choice questions with explanations.
Identify sections that require deeper review.

Reflection Prompts

Which concept from this lecture do I likely misunderstand?
Where might I be confusing similar ideas?
How does this concept apply in real-world situations?
What would be hardest to explain to someone else?
What study strategy best matches this material?

Appendix C

AI Prompts for Learning, Reflection, and Career Development

Artificial intelligence can strengthen learning when used intentionally. These prompts are designed to clarify course content, organize study systems, support reflection, strengthen writing, and articulate professional growth.

Understanding Course Content

Explain this concept in simple language, then explain it again at a deeper level.
Create an analogy that helps explain a topic.
Identify common misunderstandings students have about a concept.
Break a chapter into the most important ideas and explain why they matter.
Ask questions that test understanding of a topic.

Study Planning

Create a seven-day study plan for an exam or course.
Turn a syllabus into a semester roadmap.
Build a weekly schedule based on deadlines.
Break a large assignment into smaller steps.
Estimate how long it will take to master a topic.

Metacognition and Self-Assessment

Ask reflective questions about exam performance.
Turn instructor feedback into a growth plan.
Identify study habits that may limit performance.
Create a weekly academic self-check.
Identify patterns in study behavior.

Writing Development

Review a paragraph for clarity and suggest improvements.
Suggest questions that could challenge an argument.
Help outline an essay before writing.
Suggest ways to strengthen a thesis statement.
Create a revision checklist from an assignment rubric.

Career Identity

Identify professional skills developed in a course.
Translate a group project into interview strengths.
Identify transferable skills from managing deadlines.
Describe academic growth this semester.
Conduct a mock interview and provide feedback.

Responsible Use Reminder

Artificial intelligence should support learning rather than replace original thinking and effort.

Appendix D

Weekly Persistence Reflection

Weekly Learning to Stay Reflection

What was the most important concept I learned this week?
What study strategy worked best for me?
Where did I struggle academically?
What support did I use or could I use next time?
What professional skill did I develop this week?
What is one commitment I will make for next week?

Appendix E

First-Generation Hidden Curriculum Navigation Toolkit

The hidden curriculum refers to the unspoken expectations and practices that experienced students often learn informally. The following questions help make these expectations visible.

Where do I feel uncertain about how college works?
What expectations do professors assume students already understand?
Have I used office hours, tutoring, or advising resources yet?
What academic habits do successful students around me practice?
What hidden rule about college have I learned this semester?

Seven Vectors Reflection

Developing competence – What academic or intellectual skills am I strengthening?
Managing emotions – How do I respond to academic stress?
Moving toward interdependence – When do I seek help?
Developing mature relationships – How am I building supportive relationships?
Establishing identity – How is college shaping how I see myself?
Developing purpose – What goals motivate my effort?
Developing integrity – How do my values influence my academic choices?

Figure 2

Chickering's Seven Vectors of Development

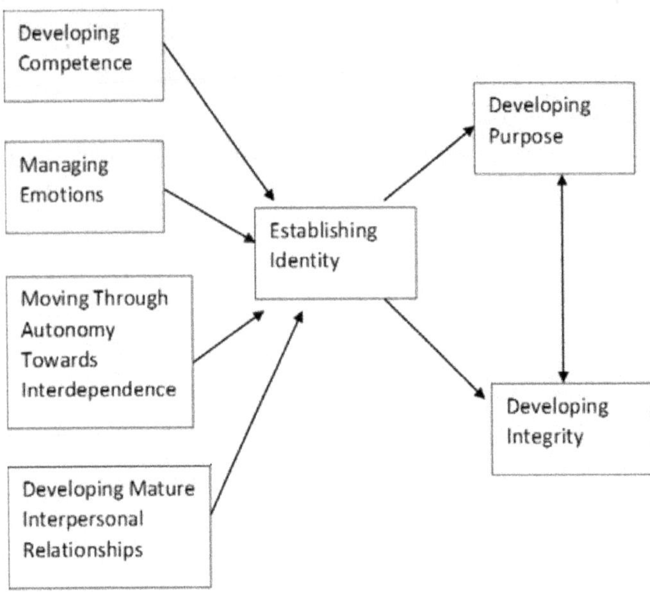

Figure 3

Hybrid Model (Tinto & Chickering)
Conceptual model combining environmental integration with student identity development.
Student Development (Chickering)
Institutional Environment (Tinto)

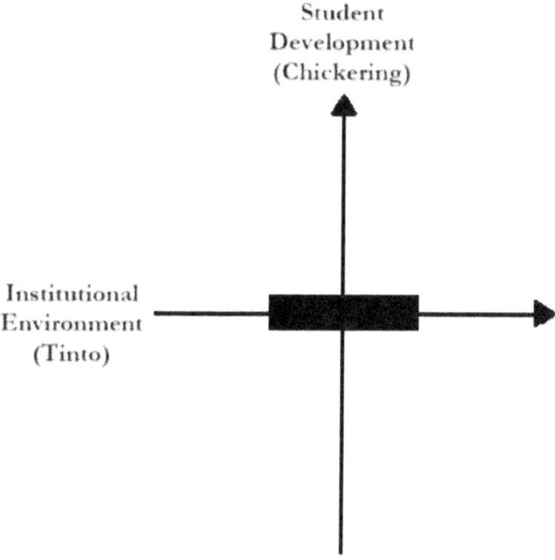

Figure 4

Learning to Stay Persistence Model

Modernized conceptual illustration aligned with the Learning to Stay framework.

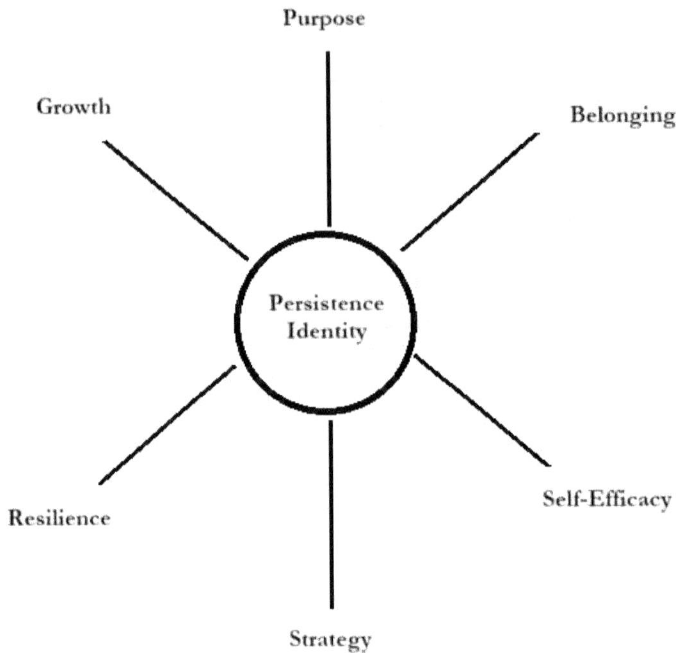

Textbook Mastery Using the 5Ws and H

When reading a textbook, do more than highlight or reread. Use the **5Ws and H** to actively question the material. This approach turns passive reading into deeper understanding.

Who is involved in the concept or theory?
Identify the key people, groups, or researchers connected to the idea. This may include the theorist who developed it, the population it applies to, or the individuals affected by it.

What is the main idea?
Summarize the concept in your own words. If you had to explain it to a classmate in two sentences, what would you say?

When does the concept apply?
Consider the situations, time periods, or conditions where this idea becomes relevant. Some theories apply in specific contexts rather than everywhere.

Where is it used or observed?
Think about real-world environments where the concept appears. This could include workplaces, classrooms, communities, organizations, or historical events.

Why does it matter?
Explain the significance of the concept. Why do scholars study it? How does understanding it change how we think about a problem or situation?

How does it work or connect to other ideas?
Look for relationships between concepts. Ask how the theory operates and how it connects to ideas from other chapters, lectures, or courses.

About the Author

Dr. Daniel E. Haupt is an educator, researcher, and community leader dedicated to helping students persist and thrive in higher education. He holds an EdD in Organizational Leadership, along with an MBA, bringing both scholarly rigor and practical wisdom to his work with students.

As the Executive Director of Denver Destiny Community Development Center, Dr. Haupt leads workforce development initiatives and educational programs serving first-generation college students and underserved communities. His doctoral research focused on the persistence of first-generation college students in high-demand fields, and the student voices in this book are drawn directly from that research.

Dr. Haupt is the founder of Destiny Leadership University and has spent over four decades in educational leadership, from the classroom to the boardroom. He is passionate about making the hidden curriculum of higher education visible and equipping students with the tools they need to navigate college with purpose and dignity.

Dr. Haupt lives in Denver, Colorado, with his wife Millicent. They have been married for over 37 years and have six adult children.

Connect with Dr. Haupt at: www.danielhaupt.com

www.ingramcontent.com/pod-product-compliance
Lightning Source LLC
LaVergne TN
LVHW010646110826
845149LV00014B/2975